MANAGING EXPORT MARKETING

Managing Export Marketing

Bernard Katz

Gower

© Bernard Katz 1987

Published by
Gower Publishing Company Limited,
Gower House,
Croft Road,
Aldershot,
Hants GU11 3HR
England

British Library Cataloguing in Publication Data
Katz, Bernard
  Managing export marketing.
  1. Export marketing
  I. Title
  658.8'48   HF1009.5

ISBN 0 566 02659 7

Printed in Great Britain at the
University Press, Cambridge

Typeset in Great Britain by
Guildford Graphics Limited, Petworth, West Sussex.

Contents

Foreword

by J.R. Wilson, MA, MIE., Director-General, Institute of Export

This book is an invaluable guide to any businessman or student who wishes to acquire a comprehensive knowledge of how to export. The businessman will find it easy to use as a reference book. The student and others wishing to learn about exporting will find the questions and answers at the end of each chapter most helpful.

The message which comes loud and clear from this book is that all existing and potential exporters who wish to increase their chances of success should make themselves thoroughly familiar with all the technical aspects of exporting and carry out their market research in a systematic manner.

There is no mystery attached to exporting and no one in the manufacturing or service industry who believes he has a product of interest to overseas markets should be reluctant to develop export business. There are many sources of free advice and information and they are clearly listed and explained in the book.

The chapter on appointing agents and distributors is particularly helpful to businesses that are not familiar with the procedures for selecting parties to act for them in overseas markets. The examples of agency agreements have been well chosen and will assist exporters to draw up suitable agreements with the help of appropriate advisers. The need to support and monitor the performance of agents is not neglected and there is a useful guide to training. It is also very gratifying to find a book that deals satisfactorily with licensing agreements, which when properly managed enable companies to consolidate their position in a market.

I am delighted that Bernard Katz has written this book as I believe it is a valuable addition to the literature available for all those concerned with exporting.

Preface

This book is intended for those who want to start exporting. It answers the question 'How do we find export customers?' The book is also useful to those who have slightly scratched the global surface but want to do better. Perhaps there are more cost-effective channels of selling overseas? Are there advantages in selling through a combination of channels? Is export business already being obtained from within the home market?

The early pages explain the difference between marketing and selling. A good salesman, very likely, is able to take a home-market product and sell it overseas as it stands. If the product is marketed, so that the customer gets what the customer really wants, export orders are bigger and repeated. How to market goods and services is described. The emphasis is primarily on the different channels of distribution that are open to the exporter to use. How to set a price, how to advertise and how to develop the product until it is absolutely right, are explained; but each discipline warrants a separate book.

There are certain export terms, and some details of established financial practices and methods of shipping and packaging that need to be learnt by the exporter, if he is to do business effectively. These are provided.

Sometimes, unsolicited export orders arrive in the post. But exporting does not often just happen in that way. The right market is found by research and application and very hard work. Market research expertise can be bought from specialist agencies. It is also possible for the exporter to do the research. How to start researching, where to look and

what to look for are described in Chapter 3. A must for
the exporter follows in Chapter 4. It is essential to take advantage of the considerable expertise and the technical and
financial support available from government sources.

A question-and-answer format is adopted throughout the
book. It is designed to provide the businessman and the
student with an easy signpost to matching a specific company
product or service to an appropriate export-marketing tactic.
Sometimes, the 'test' questions that are asked are open-ended
questions. The reader's answers to such questions will not
necessarily be the same as those provided in the text.

Checklists provide a structure for the exporter's 'How?'
– and the Appendices supply the names and addresses of
useful organizations.

My warmest thanks go to Michael Jackson for letting me
share his knowledge of exporting; and I am most grateful
to John Conacher of Hanovia Ltd and John Redfern of L.G.
Harris and Co Ltd for permission to make use of their company documents. Not least I acknowledge my indebtedness
to the bubbling interactive skills and humour of the many
export managers I now meet in the classroom.

Bernard Katz

List of figures

1 The marketing context

Before reading this chapter, answer the following test questions. The answers are worked through in the text. Question and answer are collected together at the end of the chapter as a summary.

QUESTIONS

What is the meaning of the marketing function?

What is understood by the international marketing mix?

In export markets what are the factors that are beyond the control of the marketing manager?

What is the exporter's first step in adopting the marketing function?

What arguments favour exporting home-market products in unchanged format?

What arguments influence an exporter to differentiate his export product from that selling in the home market?

What marketing tactics are open to an exporter in respect of the pricing of goods?

Chapter 1 synopsis

- A definition of marketing
- Controllable variables
- External market forces
- Getting started
- Evaluating product policy
- Pathways to profit

A DEFINITION OF MARKETING

Question   **What is the meaning of the marketing function?**

Marketing means treating the customer as No. 1, and the marketing function is primarily concerned with customer orientation. The customer is provided with goods and services that he or she really wants.

Business was not always like this. The marketing concept has only dominated business thinking since about the end of the Second World War. Before that time the manufacturer was No. 1. The manufacturer knew best. He designed and made products that he considered were just right for customers, old and new. Products were *sold* to customers. Big business was Selling – with a capital *S*. The sales concept was dominant. If one customer does not buy, another is found.

But in the market-place natural constraints to trade arise. Sales slow down, or cease, as a product reaches the final stage of the product life-cycle. Big business does not want to stop when this happens, so it resolves the problem by switching to another product. It has lots of products. The sales concept is reinforced. Business becomes product orientated. With a large number of bigger and better products, more sales can be achieved.

But with an extensive product range there are new problems. Not every product, product size or product quality is successful. They should be, but the range is not made up entirely of winners. If it were, all businesses would expand. Everyone would be rich.

Trying to get all the products in a range right, is the beginning of marketing. All the manufacturer has to do is to make products that customers want to buy. If the product is right, customers are going to buy even when the sales techniques are all wrong.

Marketing involves finding out what the customer wants. Finding out is called *market research*. But not every customer wants every product. Around the world there are millions of customers. They have millions of needs. It is possible to identify groups of consumers – the buyers – sharing identical needs. Marketing entails identifying those groups. The groups are called *market segments*.

There are other activities that are an integral part of marketing. It is not enough to identify customers and potential customers, and find out what they want. The right product has to be developed and produced. It has to be promoted to motivate the customer into buying. It has to be packaged to attract and to protect. The product has to be offered for sale in places where contact with customers is facilitated. The price of the product or service has to be such that the customer is able and prepared to buy, notwithstanding the attractions of competitive products. And marketing includes selling. Selling is an important part of the marketing function, although the two are not synonymous. There has to be a profit too.

There are many definitions of marketing. Most say approximately the same thing, the differences being a function of the literary style or academic position of the author. The definition that is now given is not intended to replace and reject all others. The objectives are to summarize current marketing thought and to offer a working definition. The marketing function has three fundamental aspects:

- identifying the needs of buyers and potential buyers in their market segments
- satisfying those needs by supplying the appropriate product or service
- making a profit.

CONTROLLABLE VARIABLES

Question What is understood by the international marketing mix?

In the market-place many forces are at work. Exporters from overseas, and importers, vie with local manufacturers to capture the business of the buyers. There are a number of variables that the export marketing manager controls. It is by manipulating these variables that the exporter's objectives are achieved. The variables are *product, price, place, promotion* and *service*. They are known as the four Ps and an S. They are the international marketing mix.

Figure 1.1 shows the marketing mix in diagrammatic form. The starting point is consumer needs. Consumer needs is a generic term covering all the needs that buyers have – from aeroplane tickets to zoological garden fencing. Needs are differentiated into smaller and more precise categories known as market segments. Within a segment all of the potential buyers have identical needs.

Between consumer needs and the interacting four Ps and an S is market research. Research quantifies and qualifies the nature of buyer needs. It is also an important tool for monitoring the effectiveness of the need satisfaction process. Whenever it is ascertained by research that needs are not totally satisfied, the marketer must develop and produce the right product or service to meet the demand still available.

Product

The exporter considers the product on a number of levels – life-cycle, design, quality, technology, usage patterns.

Figure 1.2 illustrates the four stages of a product life-cycle – launch, growth, maturity and decline. Sometimes, when falling sales indicate that the product is in its decline stage, vigorous promotion achieves a second peak. This is illustrated in Figure 1.3. Profitability is eroded by the cost of the extra promotional activities, and the manufacturer must make a careful judgement as to the most appropriate marketing policy.

Through market research, and by experience and commer-

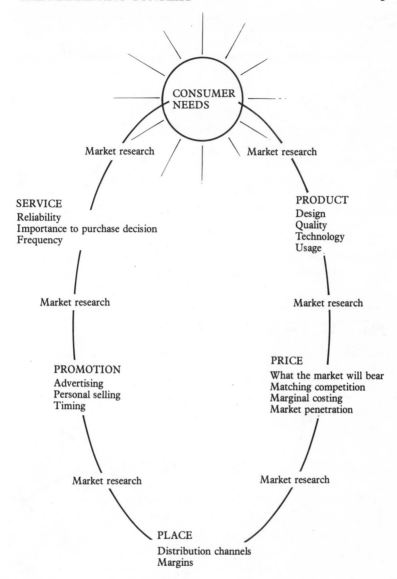

Figure 1.1 Component factors of the marketing mix four Ps and an S

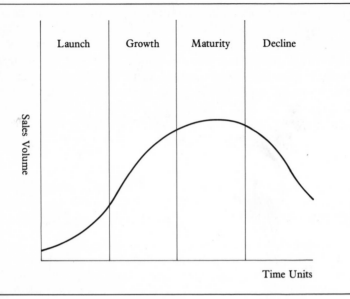

Figure 1.2 Product life-cycle

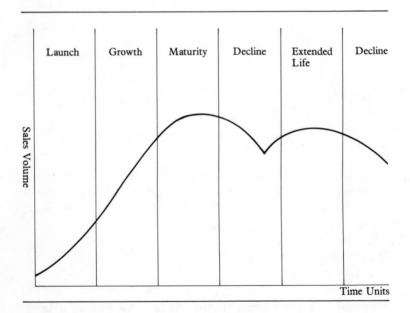

Figure 1.3 Extended product life-cycle

cial judgement, the manufacturer identifies the needs of potential customers. What product format is right for the particular export market? Is there value, for example, in preparing a marketing launch campaign when the generic product is in the decline stage? How closely do the levels of design and quality match the technology? Some export business can be achieved when the product match is partly right. Bigger business comes when everything is right.

Price

Getting the price right results from knowing what goes on at the place where the goods are sold. That is the starting point for research. There are a number of interacting factors:

- competitor prices
- whether price means status or value to the buyer
- margins of profit necessary with the channels of distribution
- exporting company objectives
- how quickly research and development costs are to be recovered
- whether profitability is more important than market penetration
- whether prices are designed to pre-empt competitor strategies.

If the pricing is 'wrong', there is no one to scold the exporter. It simply means that profits are lower than they might be.

Place

Place covers all the distribution paths from the manufacturer to the consumer. A customer buys the product from a number of different channels – by mail order, from shops, from street traders, from agents or distributors, from depots, from itinerant salesmen. There are many distribution channels. Within these channels there are varying discount structures and margins operating for the middlemen involved. The manufacturer or the supplier must decide which distribution channel or channels are appropriate to the product. More than one channel is often used. An important aspect is whether after-sales service is a factor in the purchase decision. But there is always flexibility. For example, the exporter can sell directly into an overseas market by direct visit, or sell through appointed agents.

Alternatively, a manufacturer can export without ever leaving the home country. One option is to supply bulk production to an 'own label' manufacturer overseas, who markets and distributes the goods under his own livery.

Promotion

Promotion is the 'how' of making the customer buy. Importers do not beat a path to the door of the mousetrap manufacturer unless they are persuaded that they should do so. An essential component of promotion is advertising. So is PR. In some cases where there is a relatively small advertising appropriation, PR can be used more effectively than a limited advertising campaign. An example is the house magazine of a food manufacturer, given free to customers and to retail outlets.

Service

Service is the spectrum of activities designed to enhance the customer expectation and enjoyment of product benefits. With industrial products – those that are purchased in order to produce an end product – the effectiveness of product performance is usually a function of service input. Service in respect of consumer goods – those that are consumed by the buyers – is remote from the product itself but is significant in respect of the total environment in which the product is offered to potential customers.

EXTERNAL MARKET FORCES

Question In export markets what are the factors that are beyond the control of the marketing manager?

A manufacturer of men's toiletries may export the same product to Washington, Lagos and Singapore, but those markets differ widely from each other in many respects. In general terms the problems met in those markets by the exporter are classified under four headings. They are illustrated in Figure 1.4.

Competition

The exporter cannot control the strategies and tactics of competitors. He can predict competitive strength, and the more effectively market research feedback is maintained, the more accurate is the projection. For example, a pricing level established in an export market by a competitor may be, realistically, costs plus profit. It can also be a dumping price designed to frighten off other exporters and to offload excess capacity. Research data on the competitor's pricing in different world markets may indicate the true situation.

Cultural environment

There is a common language in Lagos, Washington and Singapore but there are also different, local languages in two of the markets. Around the world, people eat, talk, sleep, travel and relax in different ways. Social and family codes are different. Life-styles differ. And so do the ways in which the consumers buy. The exporter cannot control all these different behaviour patterns. But he should find out what they are, through market research, and adapt his product to the most acceptable format.

An example of the exporter who did not research adequately is the detergent manufacturer who launched his detergent powder into the Middle East. The promotion was by means of three cartoon pictures. The first picture depicts the housewife with a basket of dirty clothes. In the second picture the clothes are washed in the manufacturer's detergent powder. The third picture is a neat set of sparkling clothes, radiantly clean. The exporter did not discover until too late that the local population reads from right to left.

Legal constraints

There are laws in most markets relating to health, safety,

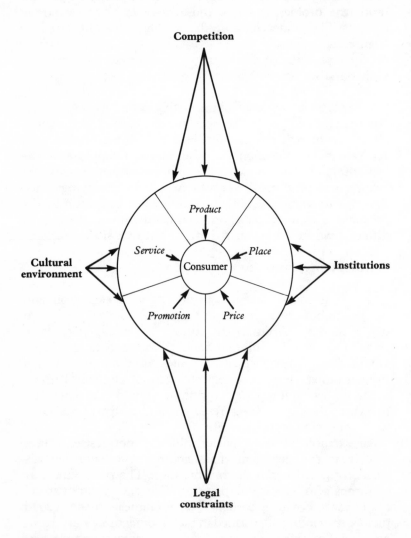

**Figure 1.4 Controllable and uncontrollable variables
of the international marketing mix**

packaging, labelling, transport modes, methods of payment, import control and documentation. There are many restrictions. For example, in Middle Eastern markets exporters can sell only through the medium of an agent who is a native of the country. Another example is in respect of advertising in Germany. No superlatives are allowed in the advertising copy.

Institutions

Institutions are commercial and public organizations that reflect awareness and support of the rights of the consumer. In the United Kingdom, the John Lewis group, and more recently Boots Ltd, proclaim the offer of exceptional value to customers. If identical goods are offered elsewhere at lower prices than in the company stores, both companies offer to refund the difference between purchase prices, without query.

GETTING STARTED

Question **What is the exporter's first step in adopting the marketing function?**

To market successfully, a company must know three things:

- what it is capable of doing
- where the best use of its resources lies
- the nature of the customer's needs.

The question is asked 'What business are we in?' This is not a once-only question. It should be asked every six months throughout the life of the company. Professor Theodore Leavitt, in an article 'Marketing Myopia', tells of one company that did not ask that question. A Boston self-made multi-millionaire consigned his heirs to everlasting poverty. He founded and built his fortune on an electric tramway corporation. He stipulated in his will that the family share interest in his empire must never be sold. There will always be, he wrote, a demand for electric suburban tramway systems. Shortly after his death the internal combustion engine was invented. It brought the car and the motor bus. It also brought the demise of his corporation.

If the Boston millionaire had asked the question 'What business am I in?' there are two answers he might have given: (1) the company is in the business of making electric tramway systems, or (2) the company is in the business of transporting passengers and freight from point A to point B. When the exporter asks the second question the answer must relate to the function, not the product. The reason is that consumer needs change. Technology changes. Fashions change. Products in high demand fall out of favour. There is always a complex interaction of market forces, and the marketer has to monitor change. Otherwise the momentum of company activities may sustain business in the short term but not over an indefinite period. The question 'What business are we in?' answered correctly, alerts the marketer to necessary changes of direction. Ernest Dichter's answer to that question applied to the cosmetics industry is now well known: 'The cosmetics manufacturer is in the business of selling hope.'

EVALUATING PRODUCT POLICY

Question What arguments favour exporting home-market products in unchanged format?

Exporting demands commitment. Great rewards are open to the exporter – but only after effort has been made. Aberdeen is over 500 miles from London. Amsterdam is less than half the distance. But it is easier for the London merchant to do business with Aberdeen, in his home market, despite the increased distance. Sales costs are less. He has more control over credit risk. Market feedback is more readily available.

So any aspects of exporting that facilitate the exporter's task are very welcome. The following factors favour a standardized home-trade and export product

- There are economies of scale when existing production capacity is utilized.
- Absence of new research and development costs.
- The inventory costs of back-up for an existing product range are less when no extra products are added.
- Less component-part stocks are required.

- The technological content of the product remains the same, dispensing with the need for additional research, expertise and training.
- In respect of consumer goods particularly, consumer mobility is a significant factor. Buyers of the product in the home market are pleased to be able to purchase the same product when abroad that they have been accustomed to using at home. Cigarettes, chocolates, snack foods are examples.
- Even where there are wide cultural differences between markets, some segments within those markets are similar and have identical needs. Denim jeans and pop music are two products whose buying segments exist in many markets.

PATHWAYS TO PROFIT

Question **What arguments can influence an exporter to differentiate his export product from that selling in the home market?**

With a standarized product the exporter has to be prepared to tackle a number of markets to generate an acceptable volume of business. When the product is differentiated to match local market needs, the exporter is able to select a market – and a nearer one is better than a distant one – and consolidate his company's presence in that market. Certain factors encourage the ´exporter to differentiate his product. Those factors are:

- local life-styles: patterns of behaviour differ from those in the home market, and consumer tastes are different
- limited purchasing power
- poor maintenance standards
- low labour costs: the technology of some products attractive to Western tastes are designed to save the user time and effort; thus when labour in the importing country is cheap, the impact of such products in their home-market format is diminished.
- limited end-user skills.

For some world markets, the exporter has no choice. If

he wants to do business there, there are certain factors requiring mandatory differentiation of the product, to comply with local requirements. Those factors are:

- legal requirements: specific health or safety requirements are laid down
- tariff restrictions on imports: tariffs carry product specifications with which all goods must comply
- weather conditions
- political considerations: government policy demands a set minimum contribution of local product or skills
- technology: many markets have set ways of solving technical problems. The exporter must comply with local precedent.
- packaging: compulsory standards are set in some markets. In New Zealand, for example, no timber content is permitted in packaging unless the timber has been treated against bug infestation.

HOW MUCH TO CHARGE

Question **What marketing tactics are open to an exporter in respect of the pricing of goods?**

There are a number of options open to the exporter in respect of pricing. Which tactic is correct at any given time is a matter of judgement. Pricing in a less effective way simply translates into smaller profits. The starting point can be the pricing policy adopted by many in the home market:

Cost plus To manufacturing costs, plus delivery costs if applicable, is added the percentage mark-up reflecting profit required. This approach to exporting is hardly adventurous. There are often risks attached to the export transaction not present in home-trade business.

What the market will bear Test-marketing establishes the highest price level at which the product is readily accepted.

Market skimming A high price is set to take a large profit from those buyers with an immediate interest in the product. Subsequently, pricing is set at a lower level to attract a larger buying segment. Meantime there has been an opportunity to gauge market reaction and to set up production capacity.

Marginal costing The price is set to recover variable costs plus profit only. This makes the offer price attractively low and competitive. Marginal costing is appropriate only for limited production capacity and where fixed costs are covered elsewhere. If substantial business is taken, it is not possible to set up additional production lines because fixed costs have not been covered.

Loss leader The price is set at a very low level, possibly at cost, in order to establish a relationship with buyers. Traditionally, Japanese shipbuilding costs have been the lowest of all countries. Profitability comes later. Japanese bunkering and refurbishment costs are amongst the highest charged.

Price lining The price is kept constant and is not increased over successive periods. The quality of the product or the quantity per unit is reduced. Examples are a bar of chocolate or a box of matches.

Diversionary pricing Pricing levels are set to develop a value image of the product.

Offset price A low price is set with profit being earned on extra items.

Tie-in price A similar tactic to the loss leader: relatively low product price is conditionally tied to the purchase of other colours, sizes, qualities or products.

Discrete pricing level Prices are pitched to known decision-making levels. This tactic has specialist but limited application.

Early cash recovery Prices and discounts are set to attract early payments. The tactic may be used when an exporter is apprehensive of political change that may jeopardize credit security. It is also appropriate when cash-flow difficulties arise.

SUMMARY

Question **What is the meaning of the marketing function?**

Answer The marketing function has three fundamental aspects:

- identifying the needs of buyers and potential buyers in their market segments
- satisfying those needs by supplying the appropriate product or service
- making a profit.

Question **What is understood by the international marketing mix?**

Answer The international marketing mix describes the variables within the control of the marketer, namely product, price, place, promotion and service.

Question **In export markets what are the factors that are beyond the control of the marketing manager?**

Answer There are four variables beyond the control of the marketing manager. They are competition, the cultural environment, legal constraints and institutions.

Question **What is the exporter's first step in adopting the marketing function?**

Answer The first step towards successful marketing is to ask the question 'What business am I in?' The objective is to identify:

- the nature of customers' current needs
- what the company is capable of doing
- where the best use of company resources lies.

Question **What arguments favour exporting home-market products in unchanged format.**

Answer The case for exporting products without any differentiation is built on economic savings. There are economies of scale and the absence of additional research and development costs. Additionally consumer mobility is a factor, as is similarity of consumer segment needs.

Question **What arguments can influence an exporter to differentiate his export product from that selling in the home market?**

Answer The arguments supporting a differentiated export product are:

- different consumer life-styles
- different consumer usage patterns and skills
- legal requirements
- environmental conditions
- technological considerations

Question **What marketing tactics are open to an exporter in respect of the pricing of his goods?**

Answer There is a variety of options open to an exporter in respect of the pricing of products and services overseas. They are:

- using a 'cost plus' basis
- pricing at 'what the market will bear'
- market skimming
- marginal costing
- using a 'loss leader'
- price lining
- diversionary pricing
- offset pricing
- using a tie-in price
- pitching at a discrete pricing level
- pricing for early cash recovery.

2 The nuts and bolts of exporting

Before reading this chapter answer the following test questions. The answers are worked through in the text. Question and answer are provided together at the end of the chapter as a summary.

QUESTIONS

What are the traditional terms of trade used by an exporter?

How does the exporter identify his goods in the trade classification statistics of other countries?

What export trade terms are used for container shipment?

What are the safest methods of payment that an exporter can ask his buyer to use?

What practical measures reduce the opportunity for making mistakes in letter-of-credit documentation?

When an importer declines to open a letter of credit, what other methods of payment still allow the exporter a measure of security?

What trading terms usually exist when the supplier–customer relationship is well established?

What financial service is available to exporters to provide prompt reimbursement against every export invoice?

When quoting in foreign currency, what protection does the exporter have against currency fluctuation?

What are the primary problems of export administration facing the novice exporter?

Chapter 2 synopsis

- Export jargon
- Describing the product
- Container jargon
- How to get paid
- Avoiding mistakes in credit documentation
- Degrees of risk in payment
- Payment terms for established customers
- The factoring option
- Hedging against currency fluctuation
- Making export administration easy

EXPORT JARGON

Question **What are the traditional terms of trade used by an exporter?**

With little effort a potential overseas customer is found by a would-be exporter. The customer wants to buy. The would-be exporter wants to sell. A deal is struck. Unless spelt out, in precise terms, the buyer and seller think of the export contract in very different ways.

The exporter considers that the goods are sold with delivery from the factory at the customer's expense. This is how the home-trade customers buy. The importer sees the goods being delivered to his warehouse. This is what suppliers do in his country.

The export contract must stipulate exactly where title to goods, and also the insurable interest in the goods, passes from buyer to seller. There are a number of 'handover' points that are internationally recognized. They range from 'ex-warehouse of the supplier, export packing extra' to 'franco domicile (named town) of the buyer, all charges and duties paid'.

Each point is described in an export sales contract by a trade term. The terms involve specific obligations on the part of the buyer and seller. They are understood by all the trading nations, and accepted by most. All ambiguity is avoided if *Incoterms* – the international rules for the interpretation of trade terms, as published by the International Chamber of Commerce – is quoted next to the trade term; for example, Incoterms c.i.f. Tokyo.

The following terms, not taking account of those used for container shipment, are those most commonly used:

ExW (Ex works, or ex factory, or ex mill, or loco)   The purchase price covers the cost of the goods only. The buyer is responsible for all charges for the goods once past the factory gates. If export packing is offered by the seller, the term states 'Ex works (export packing included)'.

FOR (free on rail)   Responsibility is to deliver the goods appropriately packed and stowed on a railway truck to the nearest rail head.

FAS (free alongside ship)   The seller's price covers cost and all charges up to the quayside next to the ship. When there is no deep water berthing the term covers all charges for the goods delivered on a lighter alongside the ship.

FOB (free on board, e.g. FOB Hull)   The exporter is responsible for all charges and risks up to the time that the goods pass over the ship's rail. In the USA, FOB has a wider meaning and must be clarified precisely. For example, 'FOB factory' means goods delivered 'free on board' the collecting truck at the plant. When it is intended to refer to a ship 'FOB vessel' is used (e.g. FOB vessel New York) – title passes when goods hit the vessel deck.

C & F (cost and freight)   In this term the cost of the goods, all handling charges and transport costs up to the port or airport of destination are included. The buyer has responsibility for insuring the goods, and for customs duty, clearing and handling charges at destination port.

CIF (cost, insurance and freight)   The shipper insures the goods to port or airport of destination and is responsible for transport and handling charges up to that point. Ownership (i.e. title to the goods) passes to the buyer when the buyer is given documents relating to the shipment, in good order. These are normally bill of lading, insurance policy, invoice of the appropriate type, plus any other document that may be specified. The insurance risk in the goods, sold on a CIF basis, and also on a C & F basis, passes to the buyer when the goods are carried over the ship's rail on loading. This is a significant point. It means that the insurable interest in the goods passes before title passes. The buyer is responsible for any loss or damage to the goods even though at the time the seller is the legal owner.

Franco domicile This term is also referred to as 'DD' (delivered domicile). The seller is responsible not only for delivery to port of destination but also for import duties and taxes, unloading, clearance and handling charges, and delivery charges to customer's warehouse. Without experience of the market, it is difficult to quote a realistic franco domicile price.

DESCRIBING THE PRODUCT

Question How does the exporter identify his goods in the trade classification statistics of other countries?

In recent years the task of understanding the systems of world trade classification has been simplified. Two main trade classifications have been adopted by most of the trading nations. They are:

Standard International Trade Classification (SITC) The revised classification has ten divisions. They are split into 625 subgroups. There are over 40 000 separate products, with further subdivisions, designated by a five-digit code number. Currently over 120 countries, accounting for the major part of world trade, submit their statistics to the United Nations using the SITC code. These statistics are published regularly. The values of goods from all countries are given in US dollars. Example classification: Commercial Vehicles – 783.10.

Customs Co-operation Council Nomenclature (CCCN) The products are grouped according to the materials from which

they are made. There is a four-digit customs tariff nomenclature. CCCN came into force when the European Economic
Community was created. It simplifies comparison of the
duties applied by different countries. This is important to
the exporter as knowledge of tariff duties applicable is essential to a realistic pricing policy. Currently there are two large
volumes to the tariff nomenclature. Although daunting at
first meeting, HM Customs officers are invariably helpful
in guiding exporters in their product classification search.

Nearly 70 per cent of world trade is conducted under tariff
headings that are based on CCCN. A complication is that
whilst the countries use CCCN for customs tariff purposes,
many submit their trade statistics to the United Nations using
the SITC code.

However, in the SITC Manual the CCCN code number
appears opposite each SITC Code. It is therefore possible
to obtain the customs import duty information for any product in any country. Example classification: Commercial
Vehicle – 87.02.

Because the classifications are by digit, the major problems
of language are overcome. In addition to the duties applicable,
the exporter has access to quantified values of exports,
imports and re-exports for all the trading nations covered,
in terms of weight or volume and dollar values.

Russia and other countries of the COMECON bloc do
not submit their trade statistics to SITC. Instead they use
a classification ETNVT (Edinaia Tovarnaia Nomenklatura
Vneshney Torgovli). However, United Nations convert the
published figures to their own SITC code to incorporate
them in their own statistics.

CONTAINER JARGON

Question What export trade terms are used for container shipment?
There are delivery terms published by Incoterms specifically
relating to container deliveries. They are:

ExW (ex works) The buyer takes delivery at the seller's
premises.

FRC (free carrier [named point]) This is the equivalent of FOB as the containers are delivered to an inland clearance depot rather than direct to the port.

FOR/FOT (free on rail/free on truck) The terms are synonymous and relate to rail transport only.

FOA (free on board airport) The term is similar to FOB, but the container is delivered to the carrier at the airport and charges paid by seller for loading aboard. Unless contrary notice is given, the seller usually contracts for transport charges to destination, passing them on to buyer.

CFR (cost and freight) This term until recently was better known as C & F

DCP (freight or carriage paid to [named point]) This is the container equivalent of the traditional cost and freight.

CIP (freight or carriage and insurance paid to [named point]) The term is the container equivalent of CIF.

ExS (ex ship) The responsibility of the buyer is to take delivery of the container from the ship, paying all costs of unloading, duties, charges and on freight costs.

ExQ (ex quay) Unloading charges, duties, taxes and fees at port of destination are the responsibility of the seller. The buyer's obligation is to take delivery from the quayside.

HOW TO GET PAID

Question **What are the safest methods of payment that an exporter can ask his buyer to make?**

There are various ways of making international payments. Some are secure; some carry risk. The options are not always with the exporter. Although removal of credit risk is highly desirable, it is frequently not possible. If a totally secure method of payment is demanded, the export contract may not be placed. In a competitive market-place, long-term credit is a powerful marketing tool. The following methods of payment are most commonly used:

Prepayment   The most secure payment of all is cash with order. It is not attractive to buyers unless they particularly want the goods. An example is when an importer wants to test-market a small sample order from an established exporter transacting large business. Without prepayment the busy exporter often has little interest in the importer's modest requirements. Where there is political instability in the overseas market, or where the goods are custom built with no resale potential, the exporter is unwise if prepayment is not a condition of sale.

Documentary letters of credit   This method relies on a guarantee of payment, promised by a bank, when specified conditions relating to the shipment of goods have been met. Figure 2.1 illustrates the letter-of-credit mechanism. The document is in a format similar to a letter. It provides total security of payment when it is 'irrevocable' and when it is 'confirmed' to the exporter by a bank of unimpeachable standing. An irrevocable letter of credit is issued by the Bank of Tokyo, Japan. It is posted to an exporter in the UK. The document cannot be cancelled by the Bank of Tokyo without the express agreement of the exporter. If a state of war were to be declared between the UK and Japan, payments between the two countries would be frozen. Although the bank is obliged to honour payments against the credit, it could not. However, if the bank in Japan has instructed a leading clearing bank in the UK, as its correspondent bank, to confirm the irrevocable letter of credit, the correspondent bank is obliged to meet the obligation of its confirmation, even if a state of war is declared between the two countries. There is a proviso. Payment, as embodied in the confirmed irrevocable letter of credit, is totally secure provided that all of the conditions set out are met precisely. Frequently this does not happen. Exporters and shippers make frequent mistakes in the documentation submitted for payment. Bankers say the proportion is very high. A figure of 40 per cent has been quoted.

If a letter of credit is not irrevocable, it can be cancelled. It can be cancelled at any time, even after goods have been shipped. But the exporter has no recourse to the issuing bank. Often, a UK clearing bank, acting as correspondent

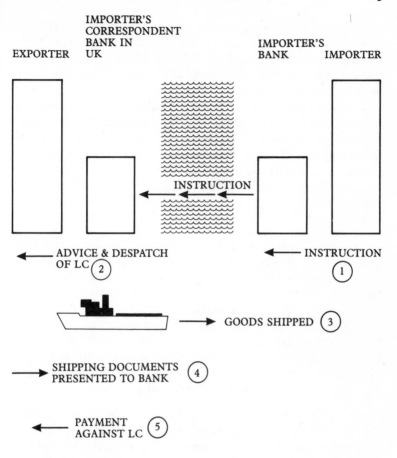

EXPORTER   IMPORTER'S CORRESPONDENT BANK IN UK   IMPORTER'S BANK   IMPORTER

INSTRUCTION

ADVICE & DESPATCH OF LC ②   INSTRUCTION ①

GOODS SHIPPED ③

SHIPPING DOCUMENTS PRESENTED TO BANK ④

PAYMENT AGAINST LC ⑤

Step 1   Importer instructs bankers to open a confirmed irrevocable letter of credit in favour of named exporter.

Step 2   Importer's bank instructs a reputable UK clearing bank to confirm the opening of a credit to exporter.

Step 3   On receipt of credit, exporter ships goods strictly in accordance with requirements of credit.

Step 4   Exporter presents shipping documents to bank for payment against credit.

Step 5   Bank makes payment to exporter.

Figure 2.1   Mechanism for opening and payment of a confirmed irrevocable letter of credit

for an overseas bank, is instructed to advise a UK exporter that a revocable letter of credit has been opened in their favour by the overseas bank. This is advice only. The UK bank is not in a position to confirm payment, because those were not the instructions.

Documentary letters of credit are subject to a standardized code of practice, formulated, and revised from time to time, by the International Chamber of Commerce. The current document issued by the International Chamber of Commerce is No. 400 and is entitled Uniform Customs Practice for Documentary Credits. Letters of credit take various forms depending on the type of transaction for which they are intended.

Transferable credit   With a transferable credit the beneficiary is able to instruct the issuing bank to make the credit available to a third party. Normally this is not possible. Provided that the terms of the credit allow partial shipments, more than one third party can be specified. With a transferable credit a middleman is able to use the security of the credit to fund the supply of goods from the third party. The middleman is able to substitute his own name, or company name, in place of the originator of the credit and to reduce the value of the credit by the amount of profit to be taken.

Back-to-back credit   These credits arise in circumstances similar to those of the transferable credit. They are particularly important where both the supplier as well as the buyer are overseas. The middleman receives a credit in his favour from the buyer. He instructs his bank to establish a credit in favour of his supplier against the security of the credit in his own favour. There are two separate credits, not one as in the case of the transferable credit.

Revolving credits   Where there is a series of shipments at intervals, the administration, and the cost of opening a separate credit after each shipment, is reduced by having a revolving credit. After a consignment is shipped and the relevant documents, in accordance with the credit, presented and paid, the credit is reinstated for the next shipment. As a safguard, the bank usually requests written confirmation from the buyer for the reinstatement.

AVOIDING MISTAKES IN CREDIT DOCUMENTATION

Question **What practical measures reduce the opportunity for making mistakes in letter of credit documentation?**

Mistakes in the documentation necessary to secure payment against a letter of credit occur for various reasons. The first opportunity for error is at the time of receipt of the letter of credit. Whether the contract is closed at a personal meeting or arrives in the post, there is a delay between signing and the advice from a bank that a credit has been opened. The excitement of the order, with its moment of pleasure, has passed. Much may have happened. Perhaps other orders have followed. Meantime the company, following normal routine, has set up the administration to execute the order. The arrival of the credit becomes, itself, part of the normal routine. The terms of the credit do not always match the agreed terms of the export contract. Perhaps the discrepancy is an after-thought on the part of the buyer. Perhaps it is a genuine mistake. Whatever the reason, the issuing bank makes payment when the terms laid down in the credit are met exactly. Discrepancies may be small; for example, 'goods to be packed six boxes per outer carton' or 'no part shipments allowed'. If there is any deviation and the exporter wishes to reinstate the original terms, the buyer must be contacted immediately by telex. It is the buyer alone who can authorise the issuing bank to amend the terms to those of the original contract.

Problems arise if the discrepancies are not discovered until too late. If the letter of credit is filed until the goods are ready for shipment, and the discrepancies are identified when delivery instructions are sought, it is usually too late. Other problems arise from shortage of time to present the shipping documents after the goods have been shipped. There is often a delay in the return of the bills of lading from the carriers. If there are any stringent time restrictions imposed by the credit, it is essential that they are known in advance so that due preparation can be made.

The path to efficient documentation is through the habitual use of a checklist. The moment a letter of credit is received, all items should be meticulously cross-tallied with a checklist as illustrated below.

Documentary letters-of-credit checklist
Place tick in the appropriate box   YES NO

- Does the specification of the goods correspond to that of the contract? ☐ ☐

- Do the quantities correspond? ☐ ☐

- Do the weights correspond? ☐ ☐

- Is the total value of the credit adequate? ☐ ☐

- Are the ports of departure and destination appropriate ☐ ☐

- Are details of import/export licences required? ☐ ☐

- Are there specific instructions from the advising bank with regard to drawing a draft for presentation? ☐ ☐

- If partial shipments are necessary, are they permitted? ☐ ☐

- If trans-shipment is necessary, is it permitted? ☐ ☐

- Does the insurance policy or certificate specify special terms? ☐ ☐

- Are there special instructions regarding the bills of lading? ☐ ☐

If Yes, OK. If No, do something about it.

DEGREES OF RISK IN PAYMENTS

Question **When an importer declines to open a letter of credit, what alternative method of payment still allows the exporter a measure of security?**

Importers without substantial resources are obliged to lodge the full value of any credit that they instruct their bankers to open on their behalf. This means that their money is tied up for many months while the goods are being manufactured and shipped. In addition, letters of credit are costly to open, in terms of bank charges. These factors combine to make the letter of credit an unattractive vehicle of payment. An alternative is a *bill of exchange* (also known as a *draft*).

When documents are attached the bill is known as a documentary bill of exchange. It allows an importer to take title to goods against payment of the bill, or against a written promise to pay in 30, 60, 90 or 180 days time. Promising to pay is called 'acceptance'. The importer accepts the bill by signing and dating the face of the bill. The term of the bill dates from that date. Figures 2.2. and 2.3 illustrate the mechanism of the bill of exchange. The parties to a bill of exchange (or draft) are:

- the drawer – who is the exporter
- the drawee – who is the importer
- the payee – the person to be paid, usually the drawer.

Bankers define the bill as:

> An unconditional order in writing, addressed by one person to another, signed by the person giving it, requiring the person to whom it is addressed to pay on demand or at a fixed or determinable future time, a sum certain in money to or to the order of a specified person, or to bearer.

For example, Security Systems Ltd, London receives an order from Wong Lim Emporium, Penang, for safety locks. The goods are to be despatched by air-freight. Agreed payment terms on a CIF basis are term draft ninety days. (Sometimes a term draft is referred to as a usance draft.) The consignment is air-freighted to:

The Chartered Bank,
Penang
a/c Wong Lim Emporium.

The goods are not sent directly to the client because possession of the goods is relinquished before payment is effected. Nor are the goods sent solely to the Chartered Bank, who are the correspondents of the exporter's UK bank. Banks are not accustomed to dealing in goods. The above styling is an indication to the air-cargo depot in Penang that the goods are intended for the bank's customer. The bank is advised that the goods have arrived. Meantime, the exporter sends the air way-bill, certificate of insurance (for the CIF

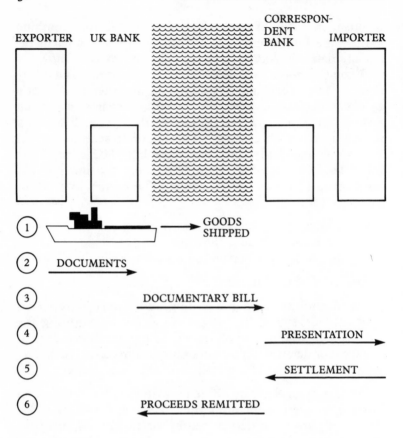

Step 1   Exporter ships goods.

Step 2   Exporter (drawer) draws draft (documentary bill) on importer (drawee)
         and submits to bankers with shipping documents.

Step 3   Bank instructed to forward documents to client for collection. Documents
         sent to correspondent bank overseas.

Step 4   Correspondent bank advises customer of bill and presents for payment.

Step 5   On payment of documentary bill, customer handed shipping documents
         representing title to the goods.

Step 6   Proceeds remitted to UK and credited to account of exporter less charges.

**Figure 2.2   Mechanism for presentation and payment
of a documentary sight bill of exchange**

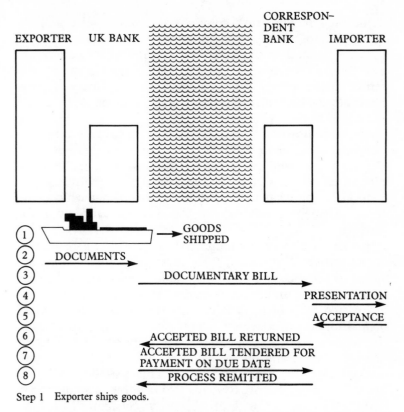

Step 1 Exporter ships goods.

Step 2 Exporter (drawer) draws draft (documentary bill) on importer (drawee) and submits to bankers with shipping documents.

Step 3 Bank instructed to forward documents to client for acceptance. Documents sent to correspondent bank overseas.

Step 4 Bill presented to client for acceptance.

Step 5 On acceptance of documentary bill, customer handed shipping documents representing title to goods.

Step 6 Accepted bill returned to UK.

Step 7 Bill returned to bank for payment on due date (i.e. after 30, 60, 90 or 120 days, whichever term of bill).

Step 8 Proceeds remitted to UK and credited to account of exporter less charges.

Figure 2.3 Mechanism for presentation acceptance and subsequent payment of documentary term (or usance) bill of exchange

value plus 10 per cent), commercial invoice and certificate of origin, together with a ninety-day acceptance draft, to his own bankers in the UK. The exporter's instructions are that the documents are sent by airmail to Penang for presentation to the client. When Wong Lim Emporium accepts the draft, the bank instructs the airline's cargo depot to release the goods to the customer.

In this transaction Security Systems Ltd have given precise instructions to their bankers. The correspondent bank in Penang must send the accepted draft back to London by airmail so that it can be discounted. An alternative option is to leave the draft in Penang until maturity at which time it would be represented to Wong Lim Emporium for payment.

Banks do not make commercial judgements in respect of merchandise on behalf of their customers. Instructions are taken in advance as to how the bank should respond to the actions of the importer. Security Systems Ltd have also instructed their bankers as to what should be done if Wong Lim Emporium does not accept the draft on presentation. In some markets, and Malaysia is one, importers are reluctant to pay sight drafts on presentation unless the goods have arrived in port or at the airport. This was one factor in the decision of Security Systems Ltd to agree to a ninety-day term. With a term draft, Security Systems Ltd gave instructions that if the draft was not accepted on presentation, it was to be presented again, and then if still not accepted, it was to be protested.

A lawyer is formally instructed to 'protest' the bill by writing on the face of the bill the word 'Protested' and adding the date and signature. No further documentary evidence is required by the courts of the failure of Wong Lim Emporium to keep to their part of the contract. Protesting is a last resort. Legal actions are invariably costly, even when won. In a small market-place where the business community is relatively closely knit, having a bill protested can damage the prestige of the importer. For example, an importer may have temporary cash-flow problems for reasons beyond his control. A typhoon in the area or a fire may have caused a downturn in business. Once an exporter has taken legal action in those circumstances it is unlikely that he will ever do further business in that market. It is important, therefore, for the exporter to maintain up-to-date information on the trends and stability of the markets to which he supplies goods.

With a term draft it is customary for the exporter to charge the importer interest for the period of the credit. If the bill is drawn in a currency other than that of the exporter, there is a risk of currency fluctuation. There are also the bank charges for converting the currency. Clauses are added to the bill to make the onus of responsibility quite clear; for example, 'payable with the collecting bank's charges'.

Figure 2.4 illustrates the document to be completed by an exporter when instructing the bank to present a documentary bill for collection.

PAYMENT TERMS FOR ESTABLISHED CUSTOMERS

Question **What trading terms usually exist when the supplier–customer relationship is well established?**

When trust is established through a healthy trading relationship payment is usually effected through *open-account* trading. The practice is simple. The exporter ships the goods directly to his overseas customer. An invoice is then sent together with all pertinent shipment and insurance documents. Reimbursement is made in accordance with whatever agreement is arranged between the two parties. A discount for prompt payment frequently motivates early settlement, but there are no set procedures.

Open-account trading offers no security to the exporter. Trading terms between the UK and European countries are traditionally open account. So are the terms between other member countries of the European Economic Community. But this fact should not influence the first-time exporter. Careful investigation of the credit standing of the importer is essential.

When the exporter's customer settles the trading account there is a delay before funds are actually credited. An unattractive method of payment, from the exporter's point of view, is for the customer to send a company cheque drawn

Foreign Bill and/or Documents for Collection

TO **Midland Bank plc**

Date _____

Branch _____ Branch reference No. _____

Please collect on our account the undermentioned Bill/documents (our reference number_____)
which is/are to be forwarded to

If left blank,
the Bank will use its own agents _____

Bills of Exchange_____ Tenor_____ Amount _____ Place drawn on _____
Insert sole, 2/2, etc

Documents	Statement	Invoices			Certificate of origin	Insurance policy or cert etc.	Bill of lading	Air Consignment note	Parcel post receipt			
		Commercial	Certified	Consular								
Number of copies												
For Bank use 1st Mail												
2nd Mail												

Air consignment note/parcel post receipt addressed to _____
If goods are addressed to a bank, see instructions below marked ✻
Please follow instructions which we have marked X below.
Where alternatives are listed, the alternative not applicable is to be deleted

☐   Release documents against **acceptance**.

☐   Release goods against **acceptance**. ✻

☐   Acceptance/payment may be deferred
     pending arrival of the goods.

☐   If unaccepted/unpaid protest.

☐   If unaccepted/unpaid do not protest.
     Specific instructions must be given regarding protest

☐   Collect all charges from drawees.
     these may not be /may be waived if refused.

☐   If documents are not duly taken up
     on arrival of goods, store goods
     (if possible in customs or bonded warehouse)
     and insure against :
     a. fire only*   b. all available risks*
     Claim from drawees, all expenses thus incurred ;
     if refused by them, they are for our account.
     • Delete as appropriate

Other instructions

☐   Release documents against **payment**.

☐   Release goods against **payment**. ✻

☐   Advise acceptance and due date by airmail/cable.

☐   Remit proceeds by airmail/cable.

☐   Advise non-acceptance by airmail/cable.

☐   Advise non-payment by airmail/cable.

In case of need refer to

_____

_____

_____

☐   Follow their instructions without reserve.

☐   For assistance only

We undertake to reimburse you for all charges, whether or not the collection is paid.

It is understood that the collection is undertaken by you only on the terms set forth on the back hereof.

Note
Original documents will be despatched by registered post, and,
if to countries outside Europe, by airmail at the customer's
expense, unless otherwise instructed. Duplicate documents will
be despatched after the originals by a similar category of mail.   Signed _____

Figure 2.4   Bank document providing instructions for collection of a documentary bill

on his local bank. When the cheque is received the exporter banks it. The UK bank then sends it back to the issuing bank. Funds are then remitted within the international bank clearing system. Many days have elapsed. An assumption is made that there are no exchange control constraints for the importer against sending money out of his country.

Alternatively the importer instructs his bankers to remit the proceeds to the exporter's bank. There are four options:

- Telegraphic transfer. Instructions are made by cable. It is the fastest method but is also the most expensive in terms of charges.
- Airmail transfer. Within Europe, there is no difference between airmail and mail transfer. The difference, however, for customers in distant markets is significant.
- Mail transfer. Sea-mail postage rates cost the least.
- Banker's draft. Although a banker's draft is a cheque, it is one drawn on a bank by itself. Provided the bank is reputable, an exporter can draw immediately against the draft, without waiting for the draft to be returned to the issuing bank.

THE FACTORING OPTION

Question **What financial service is available to exporters to provide prompt reimbursement against every export invoice?**

There are organizations, known as factors, who buy all invoiced debts from an exporter. In this way prompt payment of up to 80 per cent of the invoice values can be obtained by the exporter, who is charged a percentage of the sales value for the service. The other charges are interest charges on the monies paid out to the exporter until the time of reimbursement by the customer to the factor.

Most factors insist that all export business, or all business for specified markets, are covered. It is not possible for the exporter to select just those clients who are likely to be slow payers. The factor makes a non-recourse payment to the exporter against invoice and assumes the task of securing payments from the overseas clients. When payment is received the factor pays the balance outstanding less fees

due and less interest chargeable on monies paid, before settlement by the customer. Factoring can be attractive to exporters
because it reduces monies tied up in outstanding debts. It
also removes the burden of credit control and debt collection
and a measure of accounting and documentary activities. The
disadvantage is the cost of the service.

Usually the relationship of the factor is disclosed to the
buyer. If the existence of the relationship is likely to prejudice
early payment, the factor still buys the invoices from the
exporter, but the exporter invoices the merchandise to the
customer. He acts as agent for the factor on agreed terms
and pays over the monies as received.

HEDGING AGAINST CURRENCY FLUCTUATION

Question **When quoting in foreign currency, what protection
does the exporter have against currency fluctuation?**

There are many concessions an exporter must make if he
is to take good business. One such concession is to make
the export quotation in the currency of the importer. It is
much easier for the buyer to evaluate the true cost of the
merchandise when it is in the local currency – and costed
on a CIF basis. Invariably that is how the competitors quote.

There is no problem in making the calculation. Exchange
rates are published daily in the financial press. They are
also obtainable by a phone call to one of the main clearing
banks. Problems arise when the exchange rates move. There
are two options open to the exporter:

- Do nothing. With a relatively stable export market
  there will be fluctuations, but over the year the losses
  and gains balance out. There is a rule of thumb: if
  sterling weakens after a contract is struck, foreign
  currency payments show an exchange profit; if sterling
  becomes stronger, the currency payment shows an
  exchange loss.
- Hedge against currency fluctuation by entering into
  a forward exchange contract with the bank. Although
  there is a cost for the transation, it is sound business
  sense when the transactions are large.

There are two principal components of the foreign-exchange market:

- The spot market. The rates quoted for the immediate sale or purchase of foreign currency.
- The forward market. The rates quoted by dealers for the purchase or sale of foreign currency at a specified date in the future. They are quoted in terms of premiums and discounts on the spot rate. One, two, three, six and nine months forward are the most common rates. The financial papers tend to quote one month and three months. If the exporter does not know precisely when payment can be expected, it is possible to buy or sell currency for delivery within a monthly period, for example, between the second and third month from the date of contract. This type of contract is called an *Option contract*.

Example: Spot rate US dollar   £1 = \$1.4830–\$1.4845
(Jan. 23)

     one month forward   0.64c–0.61c prem.
     three months forward   1.88c–1.83c prem.

The fact that the dollar forward rate is at a premium means that in the judgement of the currency dealers, at the forward period, the dollar is stronger and the pound sterling weaker. There are therefore less dollars to the pound. For this reason the premium figure must be deducted from the spot rate to calculate the forward contract price. Many exporters add the premiums (and deduct discounts) in calculating forward exchange rates. It is a common pitfall.

A contract for the supply of machine tools to the value of \$90 000 has been sold to an American importer. Payment is by ninety-day acceptance draft. The importer accepts the bill of exchange on 23 January. His commitment is to make payment of \$90 000 three months later. The exporter enters into a forward exchange contract with his bankers. In a simplified calculation based on the above figures, the exporter

calculates that on payment date he can sell the dollar payment
for

$$£1 = \$1.4845$$
$$\text{less} \qquad\qquad 0.0183 \text{ prem.}$$
$$= \$1.4662$$

The pound is weaker after three months, so less dollars are
paid for every pound.

For spot and forward rates two figures are always quoted.
They are the bank 'buy' and 'sell' rates. There is another
rule of thumb to prevent confusion for exporters: in any
exchange transaction the dealer always has the most favourable terms. Dealers 'buy high' and 'sell low'. When selling
dollars to the bank for sterling, the bank dealer wants a larger
number of dollars for each pound rather than the smaller
number. Using the above figures, $1.4845 is the bank spot
buy rate, and $1.4830 is the bank spot sell rate.

In calculating the forward exchange rate the bank has to
have the most favourable terms. Premium rates must be
deducted. Therefore, of the two figures 1.88c–1.83c prem.,
the one which allows the bank to have the greatest number
of dollars for every pound sold, is 1.83c.

Another pitfall is met in the arithmetical calculation of
forward exchange rates. Spot rates are given in dollars.
Forward rates are quoted in cents.

The calculations when forward currency rates are at a
discount are similar to those above.

Example: Spot rate Italian lire   £1 = 2299.19 lr–2304.45 lr
            (23 Jan)

            one month forward   4–10 lr disc. .
            three months forward   19-26 lr disc.

At one month forward, sterling is stronger. More lire must
be paid for every pound. Discounts must be added.

An exporter is due to receive 90 000 000 lire one month

from 23 January. The lire will be sold for sterling. The calculation is as follows:

Spot buy rate $£1$ = 2304.45 lr

add 26.00 lr disc.

= 2330.45 lr

If a forward exchange contract is struck, the bank will sell sterling on 23 February at the rate of $£1$ = 2330.45 lire.

MAKING EXPORT ADMINISTRATION EASY

Question What are the primary problems of export administration facing the novice exporter?

A company is faced with the problem of shipping goods overseas for the first time. There are many basic questions to be answered:

What transport modes exist for sending goods overseas?

The nature of the goods and the destination are important. If the consignment is a first-time consignment, it is possible that it is a trial order. The physical size and weight may not be very large. This eliminates some of the options:

Rail transport Unlikely to be appropriate for a trial order. Rail transport is cost-effective for bulk shipment of raw materials from rail point to rail point.

Ocean transport Shipment by sea-freight is the traditional mode. Some markets have mandatory regulations in respect of the packaging. The delivery time is slower than with other transport modes. Opportunities exist for losses through theft and pilferage.

Air-freight Delivery is fast. Risks of damage, pilferage or theft are reduced. Costs are higher than from sea-freight, but with fast delivery the customer receives possession of the merchandise quickly. With high-value products the cost of the investment in 'dead' delivery time is reduced. With trial orders, when the customer is anxious to monitor success with a new product, it is psychologically opportune to deliver the goods as soon as possible.

Container transport   Containerization allows door-to-door service. Goods are stowed in large, standard-sized containers. Risks of pilferage and loss are reduced. Costs of protective packaging are reduced.

When the volume of goods to be shipped is not sufficient to fill a container there is a groupage service operated by specialist freight-forwarding agents. Small consignments from different suppliers are consolidated by the forwarding agents to fill a complete container. Suppliers deliver their goods to an inland clearance depot. Customs clearance is effected as the goods are stowed. At a corresponding depot in the export market the container deliveries are broken down for onward delivery or for collection by the importers.

Containers are loaded on to the sea carrying vessel by lift-on/lift-off methods, or on trailers for the roll-on/roll-off method. Container shipment has revolutionized the distribution of merchandise around the world. Large capital investment has been necessary at the handling ports for the equipment and storage facilities. The result is a very fast turnaround of ships. Containers are off-loaded and new containers stowed in a matter of hours. Turnaround with conventional sea-freight is much longer, being a matter of days rather than hours.

Post   Postal deliveries are appropriate for small consignments. Airmail service with a surcharge for 'swift' delivery is efficient and fast.

Express courier service   The service guarantees overnight delivery to any part of the world. Because of the personalized and reliable service, the cost is very high. Normal delivery of merchandise to a customer does not warrant the expense involved.

What help is available to the exporter unsure about shipment of his goods?

There are three major directions the exporter can take:

Refer to 'Croner's Reference Book for Exporters' This is the exporter's bible. Figure 2.5 illustrates a page from the book. Details are given, country by country, of the import requirements. Subscribers to *Croner* are sent a monthly update of any statutory changes as they are published.

Consult a freight forwarding agent The names of agents can be found in *Yellow Pages*. Most specialize in certain overseas markets, while some specialize in handling certain commodities and goods. The first-time exporter can fully rely on the expertise and guidance of the established forwarding agent. For this service he pays the agency fee. With small consignments the fees and expenses are a disproportionately large percentage of profitability. Where large business is concerned, freight forwarders compete for business as in any market-place.

Seek advice from the embassy of the importing country The commercial counsellor is able to state the regulations in force in respect of the documentation required. The British Overseas Trade Board can advise the exporter where to secure the appropriate information. The exporter's bankers are sometimes helpful too.

How does an exporter simplify his problems of documentation?

All exporters should refer to *The Simplification of International Trade Procedures Board (SITPRO)*. SITPRO has developed fast, simplified export documentation systems that use international standards. Some of the systems are:

- 'Overlays': master documents for use with ordinary office copiers.
- 'Spex 2': a microcomputer package that operates on over forty different makes of machine.
- 'Postpacks': a package incorporating one typing set only for postal despatch.

There are also more sophisticated systems for use by freight forwarders and very large companies. SITPRO offer training and provide many publications and leaflets on the wide range of export procedures, such as customs entry procedures,

DECEMBER, 1986　　　　　　　　　　　KOREA (SOUTH)

Republic in the Far East. **Capital:** Seoul. **Population:** 40 million. **Principal Port:** Pusan.

LANGUAGE: Korean.

WEIGHTS AND MEASURES: Metric system used commercially. There is also a native system.

ELECTRICITY SUPPLY: Domestic 110 and 220v, 60 cycles AC. Industrial: 3300, 5700,6600,22,000, 22,900, 154,000v AC.

CURRENCY: Won.

EXCHANGE RATE: 1239 Won = £1 Sterling (fluctuating rate).

INTERNATIONAL DIRECT DIALLING CODE: 010 82

TIME: 9 hours ahead of GMT (8 hours ahead of BST).

PUBLIC HOLIDAYS: Jan. 1-3; Mar. 1; Apr. 5; May 5; June 6; July 17; Aug. 15; Oct. 1, 3, 9; Dec. 25.

ENQUIRIES: Embassy of the Republic of Korea, 4 Palace Gate, London, W8 5NF (Tel: 01-581 0247); Consular Section (Tel: 01-581 3330); open 10-12; 2-4, closed Sats. Legalisation waiting period: 24 hrs. Korea Trade Centre, 16/21 Sackville Street, London W1X 1DE (Tel: 01-439 0501/3); open 9.30-12.30, 2-5, closed Sats.

BRITISH EMBASSY: 4 Chungdong, Chung-ku, Seoul. (Tel: 735-7341/3, 730-4566, Telex: 27320 a/b PRODROME).

CHAMBER OF COMMERCE: Korea Chamber of Commerce and Industry, 45, 4-ga, Namdaemun-ro, Chung-gu, Seoul.

IMPORT RESTRICTIONS: All imports require licences, which are granted only to registered traders, however, most items are automatically approved. Imports are made either through registered traders or the Government Agency, OSROK (Office of Supply, Republic of Korea).

EXCHANGE CONTROL: Imports are mainly financed by Korean foreign exchange. The foreign exchange banks allocate the authorised funds.

BILLS OF LADING: May be made out ''to order'' but must bear the name and address of the consignee.

CONSULAR INVOICES: None.

CERTIFICATES OF ORIGIN: Only if required under L/C terms, obtainable, gratis, from Embassy. To be presented to the Embassy for legalisation before shipment together with a C/O, plus one copy, issued by an authorised Ch. of C. (see pages 81-82f), and a copy of the L/C. For amendments to documents already legalised, amendment C/O forms, obtainable, gratis, from Embassy, must be submitted with original documents.

COMMERCIAL INVOICES: No special form. Do not have to be presented to Embassy for legalisation unless specially required under L/C terms. **Facsimile signatures** are accepted.

SPECIAL CERTIFICATES: An Inspection Certificate issued in the country of manufacture, is required for pharmaceuticals, medical and sanitary supplies and cosmetics, this must show manufacturer's name and address, date of manufacture, lot number, control number, batch number and date of expiration if subject to a limited period of efficacy. Health or Sanitary Certificates required for plants, seeds, vegetable products and livestock. Inspection certificates are sometimes called for by the government agency or registered trader for certain goods such as electrical equipment and machinery. Exporters should ascertain if such a requirement will be imposed, since the inspection costs are borne by them.

CONSULAR FEES: Legalisation of C/O £4.50 per set, extra copies £1.00.

INSURANCE: Most imports have to be insured in Korea.

Figure 2.5　Example of a page from *Croner's Reference Book for Exporters*

(Available from Croner Publications Ltd., 173 Kingston Road, New Malden, Surrey KT3 3SS. Tel: 01-942 8966)

guidelines for costing, arranging international finance, instituting export office routines, and so on.

A useful checklist for exporters is one relating to their costs. SITPRO publish a useful checklist, and this is reproduced below:

Cost-point checklist: fees, charges and other costs (SITPRO)

- Carriage to point of delivery.
- Insurance to point of delivery.
- Fees for forwarder's export services.
- Fees for import services (if selling delivered).
- Cost of covering against exchange rate fluctuations.
- Cost of SITPRO documentation sets and checklists.
- Fees for special documents, e.g. stamping certificates of origin.
- Refunds or levies for certain processed foods.
- Interest charges on credit sales, or discounts/fees on bank's up-front settlements.
- Bank fees for services debited to you.
- Insurance against default by customer.
- Communication costs: airmail, telex, telephone.

Under marine insurance cover, what risks can the exporter insure against?

With *marine insurance cover* goods are insured against specified loss or damage when in transit between agreed points. The starting point can be the seller's warehouse or factory. The delivery point is wherever is agreed within the export contract. The class of insurance is *cargo insurance* to distinguish between the cover at sea for the ships themselves.

Marine insurance is not restricted to the cover of merchandise when on the high seas. Insurance of exports by air-freight is included, as well as cover for sections of a total journey that are over land.

The terms of the export contract dictate who has responsibility to effect the insurance cover. Under a CIF contract the responsibility is with the seller. When the contract is FOB the responsibility rests with the buyer, but the seller can take out contingency insurance against the possibility of default in respect of the buyer's insurance. Responsibility varies depending on the nature of the export contract.

The terminology of the marine policy form is daunting to the uninitiated. The language, albeit picturesque, has changed little since Elizabethan times. The present-day marine policy form reads:

> Touching the adventures and perils which we the assurers are content to bear and do take upon us in this voyage; they are of the seas, men-of-war, fire, enemies, pirates, rovers, thieves, jettisons, letters of mart and countermart, surprisals, takings at sea, arrests, restraints, and detainments of all kings, princes, and people, of what nation, condition, or quality soever, barratry of the master and mariners, and of all other perils, losses and misfortunes, that have or shall come to the hurt, detriment, or damage of the said goods and merchandises, and ship, etc., or any part thereof

Some of the terms are obsolete. Some are as meaningful today as in the times of the merchant adventurers. For example, 'Perils of the Sea' is the first of the insured perils in the marine policy form. It covers the accidents of the sea, such as stranding, foundering, collision and heavy-weather damage.

Exporters are cautioned to take informed advice on the marine risks to be covered. The short introduction in this chapter is a starting point only.

It is usual to insure for an agreed value. This is between 10 and 15 per cent above the CIF value in order to cover out-of-pocket expenses involved in a loss. An alternative is for the exporter to have a *floating policy* where there is regular export trade. A total cover of a large sum, say £1 000 000, is taken out. The exporter reduces the total cover by the value of each shipment as it is made. The cover sets a limit on the risk outstanding at any one time, or on the value of any single shipment.

For insurance cover to be effected, a premium is paid by the exporter. The amount of the premium directly reflects the cover placed.

Types of risk covered

There are three major categories of cover, which are known as *institute cargo clauses:*

- free from particular average
- with average
- all risks.

Free from particular average (FPA) This category provides restricted cover. It is therefore an inexpensive form of insurance. The word average has a technical meaning in respect of marine insurance. It is defined as 'partial loss or damage'. Insurance claims under this type of risk will only be met when the goods are totally lost or totally destroyed.

With average (WA) Progressively there is more cover in this category. Marine policies are built up by incorporating clauses relating to the different types of risk likely to be met in particular shipments to particular destinations. WA policies allow for claims against partial loss. It is usual to recite in such policies the cover for various additional risks; for example, 'To pay average, including theft, pilferage, and non-delivery, hooks, oil, freshwater, sweat, and damage by other cargo. Including leakage and breakage. All claims payable irrespective of percentage'. The significance of 'percentage' is that, historically, with the shipment of certain commodities – such as corn, fish, salt, fruit, flour and seeds – claims for partial losses below 5 per cent of total value are not entertained.

All risks Despite an apparent contradiction, 'all risks' does not cover all loss or damage to cargo. The operative word is 'risk'. It implies that there must be an accident or casualty during the journey, even though it is of a minor nature, to render the insurer liable. Examples of risk are damage through stevedores' hooks, or pilferage, or staining through rain. There are certain other losses not covered under an all-risks policy, for example, losses due to delay, to deterioration due to the inherent nature of the product itself and to wear and tear. The exporter must consider carefully where the risks insured against start and finish. If there are exposed

times, or places, additional cover can be incorporated in the
policy.

Claims   When losses are suffered the first obligation of the
exporter is to lodge a claim against the carrier or any other
party contributing to the loss. Both the exporter and the
insurers have an obligation to work together to minimize
the losses that are incurred. After that the exporter can claim
the amount of the loss from the insurers.

To support the claim, the exporter or shipper must produce
documentary evidence in support. The evidence has to show
that loss or damage has been incurred, or that certain
unavoidable expenses have been incurred. It also must
demonstrate that the cause of the loss is one against which
cover is incorporated in the policy. The insurers will satisfy
themselves on the liability for the loss. They will also need
to satisfy themselves that the claimant had an insurable
interest at the time of the loss, whether directly or through
an assigned policy.

The following documents are normally required by an
insurer or an agent authorized to settle claims:

- The Policy. The document gives evidence of insurance
  and the terms under which cover is placed. If the policy
  has been lost, insurers will settle the claim but require
  an appropriate letter of indemnity for any loss arising
  out of non-production of the policy.
- Bill of lading. The document gives evidence of the
  terms of the contract of carriage. It also shows the
  carrier's receipt for the goods and their condition when
  loaded. If the claim is for total loss, the full set of
  bills of lading gives the insurers the right, if they so
  desire, of taking over priority rights of the remains
  of the insured goods.
- Invoice. A description of the goods, terms of sale,
  prices, charges, costs, and so on, are provided in this
  document.
- Survey report. Lloyd's standard form of survey report
  is usually used. This states the surveyor's opinion of
  the cause of the loss or damage, particulars of the sound
  and damaged values, and an estimate of depreciation,
  if this has been agreed. Where appropriate a landing

account is attached showing the quantity of goods that are missing.

- Account sales. This document shows the proceeds of the sale of the goods – if they have been sold.
- Correspondence with carriers. Evidence of payments made by the carriers are supported. Reasons for rejection of any claims are disclosed.
- Letter of subrogation. The document transfers the rights of the claimants against the carriers to the insurers. It authorizes the insurers to take proceedings against the carriers or a third party, in the name of the insured, if that is appropriate.

Claims always involve considerable paperwork. Delays are frequent. In the event of a claim it can be many months before settlement is made.

SUMMARY

Question **What are the traditional terms of trade used by an exporter?**

Answer The traditional terms of trade for exporters are: ExW (ex works), FOR, FAS, FOB, C&F, CIF and DD (franco domicile).

Question **How does the exporter identify his goods in the trade classification statistics of other countries?**

Answer Goods are internationally recognized under two classifications: Standard International Trade Classification (SITC) and the Customs Co-operation Council Nomenclature (CCCN).

Question **What export trade terms are used for container shipment?**

Answer The internationally recognized trade terms for container shipment are ExW (ex works), FRC (free carrier), FOR/FOT (free on rail/free on truck), FOA (free on board aircraft), CFR (cost and freight), DCP (freight or carriage paid), CIP (freight or carriage and insurance paid), ExS (ex ship), ExQ (ex quay).

Question　What are the safest methods of payment that an exporter can ask his buyer to make?

Answer　The options in respect of low-risk payments are (a) prepayment and (b) documentary letters of credit. Degrees of risk attach to documentary credits depending on whether or not they are confirmed or unconfirmed, irrevocable or revocable.

Question　What practical measures reduce the opportunity for making mistakes in letter-of-credit documentation?

Answer　In addition to taking particular care when dealing with documentary letters of credit, a checklist is helpful, covering all the important items to be attended.

Question　When an importer declines to open a letter of credit, what other methods of payment still allow the exporter a measure of security?

Answer　An alternative option to letter-of-credit payment is payment by bills of exchange. A documentary bill can be made out for payment at sight. When the bill is presented to the customer it calls for payment of the invoice amount. On payment the documents representing title to the goods are given to customer. It is also possible to allow the buyer to have credit for periods of 30, 60, 90 or 120 days. A bill permitting time to pay is called a term bill or a usance bill.

Question　What trading terms usually exist when the supplier–customer relationship is well established?

Answer Subject to satisfactory status, open-account trading is practised between well-established trading partners. Open-account trading means that goods are despatched directly to the customer, who is subsequently invoiced – either monthly or after each shipment.

Question What financial service is available to exporters to provide prompt reimbursement against every export invoice?

Answer A specialist financial service exists called factoring. The factor enters into a contract to purchase every company invoice. About 80 per cent of each invoice is paid to the exporter promptly. The balance is paid after monies have been received from the overseas customer. The final payment is nett of a factoring commission and interest charges.

Question When quoting in a foreign currency, what protections does the exporter have against currency fluctuation?

Answer An exporter is able to safeguard his payments against losses through currency fluctuation by buying or selling currency forward. The bank quotes rates for forward dealing one, two or three months ahead. There are charges for this service. If the exporter does nothing and the exchange rate moves, the exporter loses or makes extra profit depending on the prevailing rate.

Question What are the primary problems of export administration facing the novice exporter?

Answer There are four main activities that must be dealt with when goods are exported:

- physical distribution: the optimum transport mode for delivering the goods to the customer.
- complying with legal and health requirements at home and overseas: making use of *Croner's Reference Book for Exporters* or instructing forwarding agents.

- export documentation: making use of SITPRO (Simplification of International Trade Procedures) systems.
- taking out effective marine insurance cover.

3 Market research

Before reading this chapter answer the following test questions. The answers are worked through in the text. Question and answer are provided together at the end of the chapter as a summary.

QUESTIONS

What is the purpose of market research?

What are the two types of information sought by an exporter?

What are the two fundamental procedures of market research?

What criteria should guide a would-be exporter's choice of first export market?

What format should an exporter adopt to carry out research economically and productively?

Chapter 3 synopsis

- A definition
- Information
- Researching is easy
- A framework for decision-making
- How to research

A DEFINITION

Question   What is the purpose of market research?

One widely accepted definition of market research is that of the American Marketing Association: market research is the systematic gathering, recording and analysing of data about problems relating to the marketing of goods and services. There are two primary functions of market research:

- to reduce the uncertainties of the decision-making process of marketing
- to monitor and control the performance of marketing activities.

The first-time exporter can start exporting with very little research effort. A few names and addresses of agents or importers are sufficient to generate initial export business. They are obtainable from the British Overseas Trade Board. However, securing a few orders is only the first stage in developing a full overseas marketing policy. As the volume of projected business grows, the scope and depth of preliminary market research must grow too. At the high-volume turnover, multinational business end of the spectrum, market research is an integral part of the much broader concept of a marketing information system.

INFORMATION

Question   What are the two types of information sought by an exporter?

An exporter researches two types of information:

Secondary information   This is existing information, published in printed form or available from Prestel or Viewdata. For example, a British piano manufacturer is considering exporting to France. There is much secondary information he can secure from which to make a market entry decision. For example:

- total size of the French piano market by value
- identity of local manufacturers
- proportion of market taken by imports into France

- retail pricing structure
- market trends
- leading retail outlets.

This information is likely to be available from published government and trade statistics, from the piano trade association publications and from published directories.

Primary information   Ad hoc information is gathered for a specific purpose. The piano manufacture would find it helpful to know

- the nature of successful competitive strategies for selling pianos
- seasonal variations in sales campaigns
- a regional profile of the piano buyer
- distribution channels
- channel margins and discounts.

The most likely source of this primary information is the market-place itself. It is obtained by observation and through questioning retailers, customers and agents.

RESEARCHING IS EASY

Question   What are the two fundamental procedures of market research?

Figure 3.1 illustrates the procedures of market research. They are:

Secondary research

Secondary research is subdivided into internal audit and desk research:

Internal audit   Facts, data and information relevant to particular research objectives are sought from the historical records of the company. Such information is rarely neatly packaged and labelled in the way that the researcher would like. For example, there may be information on the cost of export packaging for products shipped to a particular market similar to the market being researched. Internal records may provide comparable per diem expenses for an overseas sales campaign.

The internal audit is always the starting point of a research exercise.

Desk research The total process of collecting secondary information is known as desk research, even though journeys may be necessary to libraries and sources of data and information. Desk research is distinct from those activities generating primary information. There is also a distinction between the research carried out from the home base and overseas desk research.

In addition to data from traditional sources, valuable information is also obtainable through computer-linked data transmission systems. Prestel is one such system. Viewdata is another. Access is not expensive. Entry to the system is through a microcomputer via a modem and the public telephone network. Thousands of pages of classified data and information are available at small cost. There is the Prestel fee on a time basis for information taken, plus the traditional telephone line costs. Information supplied is stored on microcomputer disc.

When carrying out desk research the exporter needs to know where to go and what to look for. Below are most important sources of information:

- embassies
- chambers of commerce
- banks
- trade associations
- commercial market research organizations
- university research organizations
- British Overseas Trade Board
- libraries
- export clubs
- trade exhibitions
- competing companies
- professional institutions
- personal contacts
- overseas agents
- shipping lines
- advertising agencies

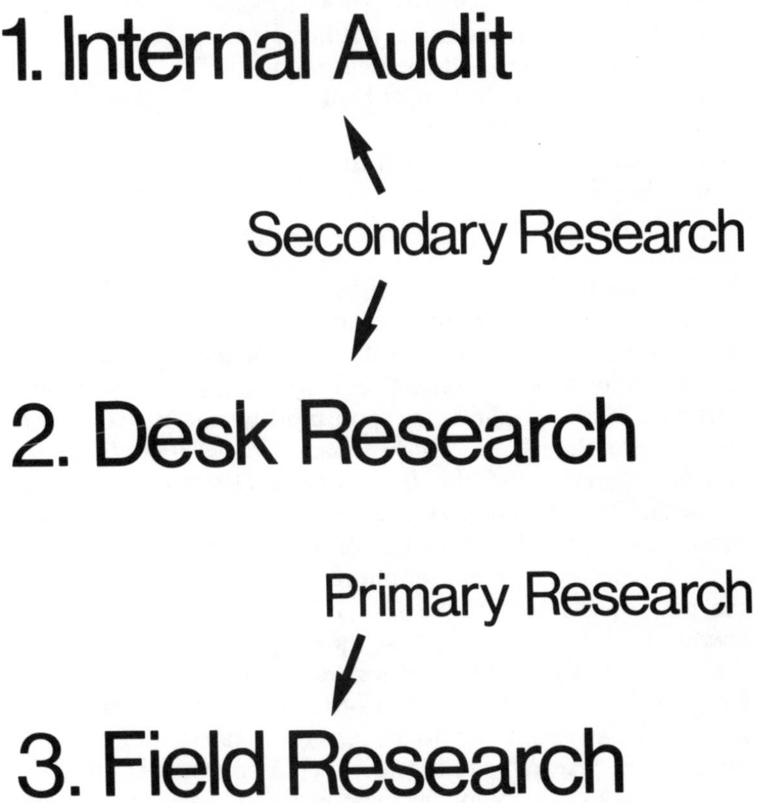

1. Internal Audit

Secondary Research

2. Desk Research

Primary Research

3. Field Research

Figure 3.1 Procedures of market research

Below is a list of the most important printed sources of export information:

- trade press
- trade publications
- published surveys
- government publications
- academic and scientific publications
- international statistical publications
- HM Customs and Excise statistics
- central and commercial banks
- competitor literature
- confederation of British Industry
- Prestel
- credit agencies

It is impractical to list more than a few examples of printed sources of export information. It is important for the exporter to know where to go to find information rather than to try to remember specific sources. An excellent starting point is with two of the publications sponsored by the British Overseas Trade Board: the *International Directory of Published Market Research* and the *International Directory of Market Research Organizations*. A short list of useful names is provided as an appendix at the end of this chapter.

Desk research demands application and resourcefulness on the part of the researcher. Other than common sense and actual results there are no signposts to tell you that you are going in the right direction. Discipline is needed too. Frequently, partially useful information is discovered, and it requires strength not to go off on a tangent. Problems occur when research findings conflict. For example, the UK trade statistics figures for the export of ball bearings to South Africa may differ from the South African import figures of ball bearings from the UK. Figure 3.2 is designed to help exporters undertaking desk research locate helpful sources of information.

Primary research

Primary research is often referred to as *field research*. The

Figure 3.2 Desk research information grid

INFORMATION REQUIRED \ SOURCES OF ADVICE	Technical Help to Exporters	British Overseas Trade Board	City Business Library, London	British Reference Library, London WC1	Confederation of British Industry	Chambers of Commerce/London Chamber of Commerce & Industry	Trade Associations	Your bank manager	Merchant banks, HP house	Relevant foreign banks	Export Credit Guarantee Department	Embassy or high commission	London buying offices	British Export Houses Association	British Standards Institution	British Chambers of Commerce Overseas	Institute of Practitioners in Advertising	Central Office of Information	Council of Industrial Design	Institute of Export	Freight Forwarding Agents
UK market information		X	X																		
Preliminary information on market	X	X	X		X	X	X	X	X		X		X		X						X
Information on country concerned	X	X	X		X	X	X	X	X		X		X		X						X
Information on market research overseas	X	X	X		X	X		X	X				X		X						X
Planning a visit	X	X			X	X							X		X						X
Direct selling to purchaser	X	X				X	X	X													
Selling to an agent	X				X		X	X	X	X			X		X						
Status reports on agents & co.'s standing	X					X	X	X	X				X		X						
Selling to export merchants				X									X								
Setting up a branch or subsidiary		X			X	X		X		X			X		X					X	
Selling through foreign buying agent				X	X						X										
Licensing & know-how agreements	X				X	X			X				X								
Credit insurance/marine insurance				X		X		X		X			X							X	X
Finance & credit					X	X	X		X				X							X	
Tariffs & taxes	X	X		X	X				X	X		X									X
Standards, patents, trade-marks & specs.	X	X		X	X				X			X	X								
Exhibitions & fairs	X			X	X																X
Promotions & missions	X			X	X											X					
Design			X															X			
Adv. & pub. & PR overseas	X															X	X		X		
Aviation, shipping & export documentation	X									X		X							X	X	
Legal problems, arbitration & international trade law				X															X		

objective is to gather primary or ad hoc information. Field research activities fall into four chief areas:

Distribution research

Information is sought on:

- Existing channel structures, for example, wholesale and retail outlets.
- Potential channel structures. These might be mail order outlets, street markets, if not yet used.
- Channel margins and discounts. What are the traditional rates? What is the scale given by competitive suppliers to the middlemen in the channels?
- Methods of physical handling. Is special packaging required for protection? Are there special requirements different from the home market?
- Alternative transport modes. How do customers take existing deliveries?
- Break bulk facilities. There are savings through bulk deliveries. What facilities need to be created?

Product research

- Concept testing. Is the idea of the product and its benefits acceptable?
- Attitude testing. How does the market see the imported product? Do performed hostile attitudes exist?
- New product acceptance. How much marketing effort is going to be required to overcome buyer resistance?
- User profiles. Who are the buyers of the product? What are their needs, their life-styles, their disposable incomes?
- Health requirements. What conditions and what constraints must be met for goods to enter the market?
- Legal constraints. Are there conditions to be met regarding safety, labelling, product size, advertising or promotion?
- Brand share. If the share is very large, relevant details are very likely to appear as secondary information in published form.

- Brand loyalty. How much marketing effort is going to be needed to gain customer acceptance?

Packaging research

- Colour. Are certain colours culturally unsuitable? For example, in China white is the colour of mourning; in France and the USSR yellow is associated with infidelity.
- Design. What designs are traditional for the export market? What contribution does the design make to promotion?
- Size. Are there legal constraints as to size? What is the implication of size in respect of delivery costs?
- Shape. Are there legal restrictions or cultural contra-indications?
- Labelling. What are the limiting factors? What makes the best promotional contribution?
- Information content. What are the mandatory requirements?
- Legal/health requirements. What are the legal requirements? Are there voluntary codes which it would be in your interests to follow?

Advertising research

Advertising research is best carried out by specialist departments of the larger advertising agencies. Sophisticated techniques, including mathematical modelling, are usually employed.

- Copy testing. What wording has the most dramatic impact?
- Media coverage. Such information is available from all media owners in published form. There is some overlap with advertising research between primary and secondary information.
- Media effectiveness. Literacy, ownership of television and radio receivers, regional coverage are all important for decision-making.

- Campaign costs. Do local advertising agencies offer more cost-effective benefits than international agencies?

A FRAMEWORK FOR DECISION-MAKING

Question **What criteria should guide a would-be exporter's choice of first export market?**

An ideal export market is one that is identical to the home market, speaks the same language and is geographically close. In the home market the businessman knows how customers think. The language is the same. He is familiar with the banking system. He has developed products that the customers want. Deliveries are made by the most cost-effective transport system.

In export markets there are additional variables to control. The pattern of commercial activities in export markets ranges from the very similar to the very different. Clearly an exporter should simplify his task and select a starting market, preferably geographically nearby, that is as similar as possible to the one he knows.

Grid for the evaluation of potential export markets

This is illustrated in Figure 3.3.

Product acceptance An ideal market is one where product differentiation is nil, or very little. The product type is deliberately set as the first item of the grid. It is used in order to identify the alternative potential markets.

Almost every country keeps a statistical record of exports and imports. In the UK this work is carried out by HM Customs and Excise at Southend. Customs and Excise will provide a breakdown of the countries to which the exporter's generic product is exported. The information is given by value and by volume or weight or unit, depending on the industry. The product is coded in the customs tariff classification. The coding is internationally adopted. When a few

	Market 1	Market 2	Market 3	Market 4	Market 5
STANDARDIZED PRODUCT FORMAT ACCEPTANCE Mark from 0 to 10 (total)					
COMPLIANCE WITH HEALTH REQUIREMENTS Mark from 0 to 10 (total)					
COMPLIANCE WITH LEGAL REQUIREMENTS Mark from 0 to 10 (total)					
IMPORT LICENCES Yes/No/some					
EXCHANGE CONTROL REGULATIONS Yes/No					
MARKET SIZE V. small/small/acceptable/ large/v. large					
OBSTACLE OF PRIME COMPETITORS Little/much/v. much					
RESOURCE OPPORTUNITIES FOR SERVICE BACK-UP V. difficult/difficult/good/v. good					
ACCEPTABILITY OF ENGLISH LANGUAGE Yes/No					
AGENTS & DISTRIBUTORS Nil/some/good/v. good					

Figure 3.3 Grid for the evaluation of potential export markets

likely markets, geographically near to England, have been identified, the next step is to approach the governmental statistical offices of those countries to obtain information about the size of the market for the product in that country, as well as a breakdown of the different import sources. By cross checking, the exporter is able to select markets where UK merchandise is known and used. The exporter also knows the competition to be expected.

Health requirements When conformity is applicable, the administrative process is likely to be extensive, in time and detail.

Legal restrictions   In the UK valuable guidance to exporters is available from Technical Help to Exporters (THE). For details see the appendix to this chapter.

Import licence   Although the licence is the responsibility of the importer, payment may be jeopardized if ordered goods are not allowed entry. If licences are applicable, quotas are published.

Import duties and taxes   This information is essential in order to calculate the local selling prices to the end user.

Exchange control regulations   If such regulations are applicable, constraints on payment may exist.

Market size   It is important that the target market is of sufficient size to justify the export effort, and that there is unsatisfied demand.

Prime competitors   Knowledge of competitive strategies, pricing and product support is essential to an export marketing product launch.

Service back-up facilities   When service is an integral part of the product offer, the facilities must be immaculate. Customer awareness of product support is an essential part of the purchase decision.

Language   Is English the accepted commercial language? Is it necessary for correspondence and promotion to be in the local language?

Agents and distributors Are there known contracts? Personal recommendation is by far the best approach to achieving effective representation.

HOW TO RESEARCH

Question **What format should an exporter adopt to carry out research economically and productively?**

The British Overseas Trade Board encourages British exporters to research overseas markets as it is the first step towards trading overseas profitably. The Export Marketing Research Scheme offers practical guidance, encouragement, enthusiasm and, in certain circumstances, financial support. For an explanation of the services available it is necessary only to write or phone:

British Overseas Trade Board
Export Marketing Research Section
1 Victoria Street, London SW1H 0ET
01 215 5377 Telex 8811074
Brief details of the support facilities are as follows:

- Using professional consultants. Up to half of the total cost is reimbursed.
- Using own staff. For research carried out to an appropriate standard, half of the travel costs and interpreter's fees are met plus subsistence allowance overseas.
- Employing a full-time staff researcher. For a suitably qualified researcher engaged in overseas marketing research, one-third of the first year's salary is paid, plus one-third of overseas travel costs, plus certain other costs.
- Purchasing published marketing research. One-third of costs are paid, but not for directories or market overviews. BOTB recommend that when their help is sought for an in-house marketing research proposal, details be submitted in a standardized format. A specimen proposal, for use as a model, based on the needs of a manufacturing company researching Middle Eastern markets is available on request from the Board. An outline of the BOTB's recommendations is given below as a guide.

Export marketing research objectives

The principal objective of research is to establish sales prospects for the company's product ranges. The main marketing problems which the company is likely to encounter are as follows:

- Whether the size and estimated growth of the market would offer prospects of substantial ongoing business.
- Whether existing channels of distribution are accessible to a new supplier. Optimum methods of distribution – or local manufacture. Selling/distribution costs.
- Extent to which the product ranges are acceptable technically and in terms of import regulations.
- The strength of the existing competition.
- Non-tariff barriers (i.e. rules and regulations, not specifically part of tariff regulations, that are limitations on free business).

Project scope

- The geographical territory to be researched.
- The company's precise product range.
- The market sectors that are a potential source of business.

Research methodology

- desk research
- field research

Field research covers personal interviews in the export territory with:

- agents and distributors
- end users of relevant products
- official and semi-official government organizations
- other information sources.

A minimum of twenty interviews are appropriate, allocated provisionally as follows:

Agents/distributors   5
End users   10

Government organizations 2
Others <u>3</u>
20

Research yield

Ascertain the current market in terms of value/volume sales. If the information is not available as secondary information, it can be gained from interviews with end users and middlemen in the distribution channels.

The future market The likely growth prospects expressed as volume/value sales.

The market structure A description of the role of agents, distributors and direct selling.

The competitive situation What are the market shares of the major competitors? Who are likely to be competitors if the market grows?

User attitudes and purchasing practice. What are

- the levels of satisfaction with existing products and with service/technical support provided?
- the perceived strengths and weaknesses of suppliers in the market?
- existing/latent demands for improvements to products currently available?
- opportunities for latchkey/turnkey services in the supply, installation, commissioning and operation of heavy equipment?
- preferred price levels/discounts/terms of payments?
- the decision-making processes in the choice of products?

Analysis of the information gained from desk research and from field research interviews allows the criteria for market entry decision-making to be defined. They are also ranked in order of relative importance:

- Products, prices, quantity discounts applicable to consumables

- product specifications
- product availability
- local representation/installation and back-up services
- lead times to delivery
- actual delivery times
- promotional mix – media advertising/direct mail/selling approach/equipment demonstrations
- ability to modify standard equipment to accommodate customer's special requirements
- speed of response to customer enquiries
- flexibility in price negotiation.

Other criteria, unique to the market, may emerge during the course of the research. With the data described above, the exporter is in a position to decide whether to commit resources for a product launch into the market researched.

SUMMARY

Question   **What is the purpose of market research?**

Answer   The purpose of market research is (1) to reduce the uncertainties of the decision-making process of marketing and (2) to monitor and control the performance of marketing activities.

Question   **What are the two types of information sought by an exporter?**

Answer   An exporter researches two types of information: (1) secondary information – existing information available in published or data form – and (2) primary information – ad hoc information that is gathered for a specific purpose.

Question   **What are the two fundamental procedures of market research?**

Answer   The two basic procedures of research are secondary research – often known as desk research – and field research.

Question What criteria should guide a would-be exporter's choice of first export market?

Answer An ideal export market is one that is identical to the home market, speaks the same language and is geographically close.

Question What format should an exporter adopt to carry out research economically and productively?

Answer An exporter should research markets methodically under the following heads: objectives, project scope, research methodology and research yield.

APPENDIX TO CHAPTER 3: ORGANIZATIONS AND PUBLICATIONS

United Nations
  Statistical Yearbook
  Directory of International Statistics
  Monthly Bulletin of Statistics
Organization of Economic Co-operation and Development (OECD)
  Economic surveys of member countries
  Financial statistics
  Consumer Price Indices (monthly)
  Food consumption statistics
US government statistics
  Statistics Abstract of the US
  Monthly Catalog of US Government publications
  American Statistics Index
Statistical Office of the European Community
  General Statistical Bulletin
  Economic Survey of Europe
  Bulletin of the European Communities
International Monetary Fund
  Balance of Payments yearbook

  • British Overseas Trade Board, Export Intelligence Service. Department of Trade, 1 Victoria Street, London SW1H OE7, 01 215 7877.

- Exports Credit Guarantee Deparment, Aldermanbury House, Aldermanbury, London EC2P 2EL, 01 382 7000.
- London Chamber of Commerce and Industry, 69 Cannon Street, London EC4N 5AB, 01 248 4444.
- Central Office of Information, Hercules Road, London SE1, 01 928 2345.
- EEC Information Unit, Department of Industry, 1 Victoria Street, London SW1H 0ET, 01 215 7877.
- Institute of Export, 64 Clifton Street, London EC2A 4HB, 01 247 9812.
- Simplification of International Trade Procedures Board, SITPRO Almack House, 26 and 28 King Street, London SW1Y 6QW, 01 930 0532.
- UK import and export statistics: HM Customs and Excise, Statistical Office, Portcullis House, 27 Victoria Avenue, Southend on Sea SS2 6AL.
- Customs Co-operation Council Nomenclature, 40 Rue Washington, B-1050 Bruxelles.
- European Communities Commission, 8 Storey's Gate, London SW1, 01 222 8122.
- Organization for Economic Co-operation and Development (OECD), 2 Rue Andre Pascal, 75775 Paris 16.

4 Government help

Before reading this chapter, answer the following test questions. The answers are worked through in the text. Question and answer are provided together at the end of the chapter as a summary.

QUESTIONS

What government help in the field of exporting is available to the small company with limited resources?

How useful are the government schemes for the company that is already exporting and needs more export orders, not advice?

What specialist help is there for exporters who have already used BOTB services to reach export markets?

In addition to advice and information, are there any BOTB publications that exporters can keep in their own libraries?

What help is there for the exporter who wants to deal with proven export markets rather than pioneer new territories?

Are there organizations complementary to those of the BOTB that are able to help and advise the exporter?

Chapter 4 synopsis

- Help for everyone
- Practical advice for practical results
- How to get even better
- Back-up publications
- Learning from success
- Complementary organizations that help

HELP FOR EVERYONE

Question **What government help in the field of exporting is available to the small company with limited resources?**

The Department of Trade and Industry provides four main groups of services to commerce and industry. Services to exporting is one of those groups. The British Overseas Trade Board is an official organization with the secretary of state for trade and industry as its president.

Through BOTB the practical skills of experienced and successful businessmen are available to help exporters, large and small alike. Much literature is available to exporters free of charge. The descriptions given below, of the different services available to exporters, are taken from the literature. The reader is recommended to ask for additional information on any of the services that can assist the export function. Help is available in the form of literature and by individual consultation with specialist market research advisers. The would-be exporter who does not really know where to start and who wants to be pointed in the right direction, has only to telephone his BOTB regional office.

PRACTICAL ADVICE FOR PRACTICAL RESULTS

Question **How useful are the government schemes for the company that is already exporting and needs more export orders, not advice?**

Successful exporting stems from a number of factors:

- sound marketing practice
- well-researched data and information concerning
  - the product: price, quality, design, composition
  - the customer: his culture, his life-style, disposable income, how he buys
  - distribution channels within the customer's market
  - political and economic market forces
- exporter's resources of management time, finance, language skills, business skills
- luck.

If even one component alone is made more effective, export performance can improve. The range of support services that is offered by the government is provided under specific subject/activity headings. Under each heading there are subdivisions. In this way the exporter is able to pinpoint the particular area where government help may reinforce the individual export effort.

The services offered by British Overseas Trade Board are as follows:

Market advice

Free information and advice on markets Specialist information is freely available on products, markets, tariffs and financial support services.

Statistics and market intelligence library Access is available to UK and foreign statistics, trade directories, development plans and other published information on overseas markets.

Product data store There is a central bank of product and industry based information about markets worldwide. Material is stored under SIC classification, which breaks it down into 3 000 headings.

Export marketing research scheme Free advice. Financial grant support is available under certain conditions.

World aid section Large projects can gain financial support through international aid agencies. Up-to-date information on the full range of agencies is available. Guidance is provided on the procedures for tendering for appropriate contracts.

Getting into the market

Export representative service Through the commercial departments of British embassies overseas, and through the diplomatic posts, reliable representatives can be found. Exporters are provided with a short list of businessmen with whom to negotiate directly. Their credentials will have already been checked.

Market prospects service Research is carried out for the exporter by British embassy staff overseas. A market report provides the names of contacts in the market-place wanting to do business.

Export intelligence service A non-stop supply of export enquiries and opportunities is available from nearly 200 British diplomatic posts worldwide. Each item is computer coded so that it can match immediately the export information sought.

Outward missions There are many advantages to joining a pre-planned trade mission going abroad. In addition to generous travel grants, there are the benefits of travelling with experienced exporters.

Market entry guarantee scheme A grant to cover 50 per cent of the cost of on-the-spot office accommodation, staff train-ing, sales promotion, and so on, is available. Repayments are made out of the export sales that are generated – but if the venture is unsuccessful, any shortfall at the end of the agreed period is cancelled.

Trade fairs overseas An exhibition stand and display aids are available at reduced rates. There are travel grants for fairs outside Europe. Participants join a group of British exhibiters at the fair.

Overseas seminars Generous help is available with costs and organization of bringing British products or services to the attention of a specific audience.

Store promotions A well organized theme promotion by a large retail outlet overseas is a source of much business. When there is a specifically British flavour to the event, BOTB support for British goods can help manufacturers and traders generate much business.

Inward missions. When representative bodies such as Trade Associations organize business visits to the UK by groups from abroad, there is generous financial support available from BOTB. Such groups are made up of businessmen, journalists and others in a position to influence the placing of business. Through BOTB your company can be included on the visitor's itinerary.

HOW TO GET EVEN BETTER

Question What specialist help is there for exporters who have already used BOTB services to reach export markets?

BOTB are aware of the different problems faced by exporters. They offer support to match the needs:

Tariffs and regulations Finding a way through the tangle of tariffs and regulations is a daunting task. It is, however, one that exporters must overcome. Experts are available to teach exporters how to master the administrative problems that face them.

Technical Help to Exporters (THE) Every country has its own technical standards. In most cases they have to be matched in order to sell in that market. THE offers advice backed by wide technical know-how and an extensive data store.

Export paperwork (SITPRO) The Simplification of International Trade Procedures Board has already been mentioned in Chapter 2. Much effort has been devoted to reducing the amount of paperwork to a manageable and efficient form. Simplified systems are available to cover every type of export.

Publicity for exports Publicity material produced by the BOTB publicity unit and by the Central Office of Information is sent to information officers at British embassies, High Commissions and Consular posts in over 150 countries. Their task is to place it with local newspapers, trade and technical magazines and television and radio stations. Newsworthy material about exporters successes, products and personnel are always welcome.

BACKGROUND PUBLICATIONS

Question **In addition to advice and information, are there any BOTB publications that exporters can keep in their own libraries?**

The exporter is very well served with booklets and books.

Hints to Exporters This is a series of booklets, regularly updated, each about a different overseas market. The appropriate booklet is essential reading before going overseas. It gives information on currency and exchange control regulations, methods of doing business, local holidays, economic factors, social customs, and practical hints, such as how and when to tip.

Export Handbook The book is a comprehensive guide to government and non-government facilities. It covers UK exporting regulations, insurance, finance, transportation, documentation, industrial property rights overseas, contact points, export awards and much else. It is available from HMSO and most leading bookshops.

Western Europe Country Profiles Separate profiles for each market are available free from Export to Europe Branch, 1 Victoria Street, London SW1H 0ET. *Marketing Consumer Goods in Western Europe*, with separate editions for Italy, West Germany, Belgium, France, Spain and the Netherlands are obtainable free from the same source.

Countertrade This guide describes the most common forms of countertrading and gives advice to exporters encountering countertrade demands for the first time.

Do You Export Your Imports? This leaflet explains Inward Processing Relief. Under this system, customs duties can be saved on goods imported from outside the European Economic Community and then processed and re-exported.

LEARNING FROM SUCCESS

Question **What help is there for the exporter who wants to deal with proven export markets rather than pioneer new territories?**

With certain markets the UK is already transacting considerable business. BOTB has set up separate departments staffed with people who have first-hand knowledge of the particular country, the people, the culture, the language and the infrastructure of industry and commerce. The departments are:

Exports to Japan Unit British exports to Japan are now approaching £1 billion per annum. There is therefore great potential for exporters. The market can be profitable, but it is not easy to penetrate without time and patience. The Japan Unit was set up in 1973 to provide specialist advice for exporters.

Exports to Europe Branch Well over half of all British exports already go to Western Europe. It has more than five times the population and six times the buying power of the UK. There is a separate country desk to help with facts, information, advice, promotional help, and with grants where appropriate.

Exports to North America Branch The USA is the biggest single market in the world, with total annual imports of £186 billion. In practical terms it is not a single market. Physically it is huge: 3.6 million square miles. It is made up of diverse ethnic groups, regional markets, principal trading areas and forty identifiable rich urban markets where quality merchandise is in demand. There are few limiting factors as far as British goods are concerned. To help the exporter the department can advise on how to get the product right, how to promote the goods, where to sell and what to avoid.

Selective Marketing: Chemical Export to Latin America There is a continuing need by most Latin American countries for a wide range of chemicals that cannot be produced locally.

BOTB's computerized selective marketing system – Computachem – helps the chemicals exporter to improve sales in Latin America. Computachem details the specific chemicals requirements of over 300 named Latin American importers in eleven different markets.

East European Trade Council The Council collects and disseminates all information that is relevant to furthering visible and invisible trade between the UK and the Comecon countries.

COMPLEMENTARY ORGANIZATIONS THAT HELP

Question **Are there organizations complementary to those of the BOTB that are able to help and advise the exporter?**

There are a number of specialist organizations able to help the exporter with particular problems:

Export Credits Guarantee Department (ECGD) This government department encourages exports by providing insurance cover against a wide range of risks. Usually the cover cannot be placed on the commercial insurance market.

Many exporters are obliged to sell overseas on credit. The length and the terms of the credit are crucial to securing business. The ECGD provides cover for the following risks in the export of goods and services sold on terms of up to six months' credit:

- Insolvency of the buyer.
- The buyer's failure to pay within six months of due date for goods which he has accepted.
- The buyer's failure to take up goods which have been despatched to him, where the failure is not attributable to any action of the policy-holder and where the ECGD decides that the institution or continuation of legal procedures against the buyer would serve no useful purpose.
- A general moratorium on external debt decreed by the government of the buyer's country or of a third country through which the payment must be made.

- Any other action by the government of the buyer's country which prevents the performance of the contract in whole or part.
- Political events, economic difficulties, legislative or administrative measures arising outside of the UK which prevent or delay the transfer of payment or deposits made in respect of the contract.
- Legal discharge of the debt in a foreign currency, which results in a shortfall at the date of transfer.
- War and certain other events preventing performance of the contract provided that the event is not one normally insured with commercial insurers.
- Cancellation or non-renewal of a UK export licence, or the prohibition or restriction on export of goods from the UK by law.
- The failure or refusal by a public buyer to fulfil the contract for reasons not arising from any fault of the policy-holder.

The ECGD, which is funded by the Treasury, acts like any other insurance company, by spreading its risks across many markets. The objective, however, is to break even rather than to earn a profit for shareholders as the commercial companies have to do. The cover does not absolve the exporter from being commercially responsible. Usually the compensation is for less than the full contract value, and the lead time for settlement is frequently longer than in commercial situations.

In addition to offering insurance cover, there are facilities for ECGD to assist the exporter in obtaining finance. By means of direct bank guarantees from the ECGD to the bank, banks will provide short-, medium- and long-term credit. The banks provide finance at a small premium over bank base rate. There is a range of situations in which funding is provided. In certain circumstances the loans are without recourse to the exporter, in the event of buyer default.

For large overseas capital projects, specific bank guarantees are arranged through the ECGD, enabling the buyer to obtain bank financing.

ECGD facilities are comprehensive and complex. Exporters are advised to seek guidance from the department directly or from their bankers. The ECGD has a regional network of offices. The addresses are in local telephone directories.

Defence Sales Organization (DSO) This organization exists to help British firms market and sell their defence products and services overseas. The DSO is part of the Ministry of Defence. It can assist companies with advice on defence market prospects on a worldwide, regional or country basis, by providing military assistance in support of sales, and in other ways. Contact:

Director of Marketing Services,
Defence Sales Organization
Room 707
Stuart House
23-25 Soho Square
London W1V 5FJ
Tel. 01 632 4826

Chambers of commerce Practical advice, help and information is available to members on many aspects of exporting. Addresses are to be found in local telephone directories. Alternatively, contact:

Association of British Chambers of Commerce (ABCC)
212a Shaftsbury Avenue
London WC2H 8EW
Tel 01 240 5831

Freight forwarders These carry out the handling and through-transport arrangement for the greater part of exports from the UK. Contact through *Yellow Pages* or:

Institute of Freight Forwarders Ltd
Suffield House
9 Paradise Road
Richmond
Surrey TW9 1SA
Tel 01 948 3141

SUMMARY

Question **What government help in the field of exporting is available to the small company with limited resources?**

Answer The British Overseas Trade Board is a government department offering practical help, advice and grant support to exporting companies, large and small.

Question How useful are the government schemes for the company that is already exporting and needs more export orders, not advice?

Answer BOTB support is designed to help exporters increase the efficiency, and therefore the productivity and profitability, of their export operations.

Question What specialist help is there for exporters who have already used BOTB services to reach export markets?

Answer Experts are available for consultation, who can help exporters in matters of tariffs and government regulations, technical standards and in cost-saving systems of documentation.

Question In addition to advice and information, are there any BOTB publications that exporters can keep in their own libraries?

Answer The exporter is very well served with books and booklets. In particular, Hints to Exporters, providing essential and practical information for different overseas markets, is essential reading before any business trip abroad.

Question What help is there for the exporter who wants to deal with proven export markets rather than pioneer new territories?

Answer For America, Japan and Europe which are exellent markets for Britain, there are specialist departments offering informed guidance and support to exporters.

Question   Are there organizations complementary to the BOTB that are able to help and advise the exporter?

Answer   There are indeed a number of organizations providing general and specialist exporters with help. Invaluable support in respect of credit insurance and export funding is provided by the Export Credits Guarantee Department.

5 Generating export business from within the UK

Before reading the chapter, answer the following questions. The answers are worked through in the text. Question and answer are provided together at the end of the chapter as a summary.

QUESTIONS

How important is it to visit overseas markets to take export orders?

What organization is primarily concerned with export business originating from public sector clients overseas?

What third-party trading organizations buy from sources in the home market, for overseas clients?

How is profitable export business organized for markets lacking convertible currency with which to make payment?

Through what circumstances are exporters able to meet overseas buyers in the home market?

What opportunities exist in the UK to export as principals through the services of third parties?

What preparations should precede the serious exporter's efforts to generate overseas business from within the UK?

> *Chapter 5 synopsis*
>
> - Exporting starts at home
> - Exporting to governments
> - Exporting through third parties
> - Exporting without travel
> - Using export specialists
> - Getting ready
> - Non-currency export payments

EXPORTING STARTS AT HOME

Question **How important is it to visit overseas markets to take export orders?**

Substantial export business is available to British companies from within the UK. Much can be taken literally from the office desk. There are government and commercial organizations buying on behalf of overseas customers. There are others buying to sell themselves in foreign markets.

Would-be exporters can assess the effort required to sell to the potential export buyers in the home market. This is then balanced against the effort and use of resources in selling directly overseas. There is no reason why the two activities cannot be undertaken in parallel. Before export business grows to substantial turnover, there is often a lead time between stimulus to the export market and return reaction. Figure 5.1 illustrates the opportunities for exporting from within the home market.

EXPORTING TO GOVERNMENTS

Question **What organization is primarily concerned with export business originating from public sector clients?**

Crown Agents is an organization that acts as buying agents for overseas governments and local authorities. It is a government department funded by the Treasury. The products are primarily industrial and capital goods, and specialist services. Buying is usually by competitive tender. Crown Agents do

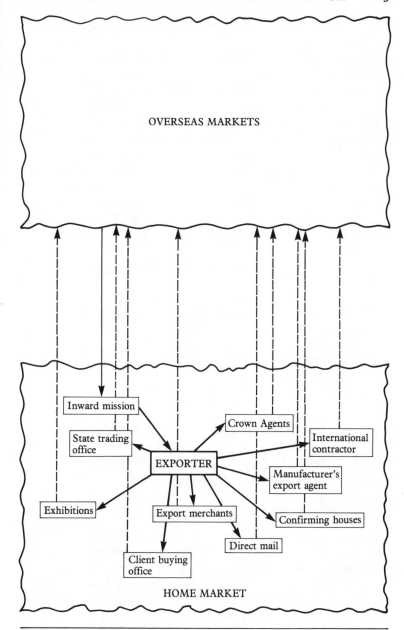

Figure 5.1   Opportunities for exporting from within the home market

not act on behalf of any private or commercial interests overseas.

Another activity of Crown Agents is acting as project manager on engineering and construction projects. For example, contracts range from the supply and installation of a television broadcast system in Brunei to the training and supply of guide dogs for the blind in Malaysia. Another contract example is the supply and installation of a complete railway system in Nigeria.

When acting as project managers the loyalty of Crown Agents lies in meeting the objectives of the assignment. This is illustrated by the Nigerian railway contract. The most competitive offer for rolling stock came from Japan. So it was with the Japanese suppliers that an appropriate contract was placed.

To register as potential suppliers, contact should be made with:

Head of Supplies Department
Crown Agents for Overseas Governments and
Administrations
4 Millbank
London SW1P 3JD
Tel. 01 222 7730
Telex: 916205

EXPORTING THROUGH THIRD PARTIES

Question What third-party trading organizations buy from sources in the home market for overseas clients?

Confirming houses

Goods are purchased by confirming houses, acting as principals for overseas clients. Payments are made to the suppliers promptly following shipment of the goods.

An order with forwarding instructions is placed by the confirming house, with the supplier. The supplier ships the goods directly to the overseas client. The supplier invoices the confirming house, sending the original sets of bills of lading duly signed by the carriers (evidencing that the goods have been received for shipment in good order). Additionally, a certificate of insurance, certificate of origin, consular invoice or other appropriate document as specified by the confirming house is included. Payment is usually made promptly to secure a cash discount.

The confirming house then sends on the shipping documents to the overseas client. A buying commission is charged to cover the administration process, working profit and interest charges. A period of extended credit – of ninety days to 120 days – is allowed for settlement of the account.

Confirming houses work with two kinds of indent from their overseas clients:

- Open indent. The confirming house has discretion to purchase goods required by the client, from whatever source is found to be expedient.
- Closed indent. The overseas client specifies precisely the supplier, price, quantity, quality and description of the goods needed.

Confirming houses specialise in the markets serviced and in the products handled. To initiate business, a quotation with samples is made to the confirming house. This is then forwarded by the confirming house to appropriate clients overseas. For repeat business the exporter is able to sell directly to the client overseas, or to the confirming house. For information, contact:

British Export Houses Association
69 Cannon Street
London EC4N 5AB
Tel. 01 248 4444.

Export merchants

Export merchants can be likened to wholesalers selling in the home trade. They buy as principals for their own account. They then sell on to their own customers overseas. The identity of the overseas customer is not usually disclosed to the supplier.

To the supplier's price the export merchant adds a margin to cover a working profit and the export costs. This reflects a difference between confirming house business and export merchant business. The confirming house buying commission varies between 3 per cent and 5 per cent depending on the industry. Merchant profits can be 25 per cent or more.

Export merchants specialise in product lines and in the geographical territories served. For information contact the British Export Houses Association at the address above. Alternatively, refer to the *Kompass Directory*, (published by Kompass Publishers Ltd, Windsor Court, East Grinstead House, East Grinstead, West Sussex RH19 1XD, tel. 0342 26972).

Export buying offices association

The Association represents the leading department stores, importers and manufacturers in most countries of the world. It advises manufacturers on the suitability of their merchandise in respect of the needs of their overseas principals. The Association has expert knowledge of the import regulations overseas pertaining to the different markets.

Merchandise is purchased by the Association, with payment being made in accordance with their terms from London. Contracts are placed at ex works, or f.o.b. prices. Members of the Export Buying Offices Association together purchase the greater part of consumer goods that are sold from Britain to department stores overseas. For information and literature, contact:

Export Buying Offices Association
Elsley House,
24–30 Gt Titchfield House,
London W1P 8BB
Tel. 01 637 0122

Exporting without travel

Question **Through what circumstances are exporters able to meet overseas buyers in the home market?**

Inward missions Overseas (and UK) buyers regularly travel in organized groups to evaluate new sources of product supply. Inward missions have already been mentioned in the previous chapter. Arranging for the exporter's company to be on the itinerary of a visiting mission is one of the services provided by BOTB.

Most of the missions are organized individually by trade associations and organizationṣ from within their local countries, regions and towns. Others are mounted at government level. Missions are of two categories: scatter missions and specifically planned itineraries.

Action: Obtain the names and addresses of overseas industry and trade associations through the relevant embassies or chambers of commerce. Make initial contact directly with the associations for planned future visits, giving details of product ranges on offer.

State trading offices Countries with centrally planned economies purchase through state trading organizations. They place contracts overseas when supplies cannot be secured from within their national boundaries or from satellite countries. There is an important proviso. The product specification must fall within the existing quota requirements. Quota planning is on five- and seven-year bases. Purchases are not made on an ad hoc basis, irrespective of need. There is a significant difference between trade with free-trading countries and trade with countries which have a planned economy. When contracts are placed, they are usually on an f.o.b. basis so that freight costs are earned by the carriers of the purchasing country.

Business, when it is established, can be substantial. Payments are usually straightforward. However, if there is a dispute, payments are likely to be suspended until the dispute is resolved; negotiations will be protracted. With small companies cash-flow problems can arise. Contracts with state trading agencies are often placed subject to arbitration, in the event of a dispute, by a body within the planned economy.

Action: State trading offices are listed in the UK telephone directories. Make contact to identify (1) quota requirements within the current trading plan and (2) local styling and address of purchasing department.

International exhibitions within the UK

Some   specialist   industry   exhibitions   are   promoted internationally. Participation involves expense and planning. But there are valuable returns. In addition to sales contacts, exhibitions attract potential agents and distributors. Another important aspect of the international exhibition is the feedback that is obtained on product innovation and development within the industry.

Action: For details of all forthcoming exhibitions refer to the *Exhibition Bulletin* (published by London Bureau, 266-72 Kirkdale, Sydenham, London SE26 4RZ, tel. 01 778 2288).

USING EXPORT SPECIALISTS

Question   What opportunities exist in the UK to export through third parties?

The specialist skills of companies and individuals can generate export business for manufacturers in the home market:

Piggy-back marketing   An arrangement is made with an established exporter of complementary products. Export orders are secured from the marketing efforts of the host company.

Example: Company A manufactures abrasives and wants to start exporting. It teams up with company B, which manufactures small power tools and has substantial export business through long-established distribution channels in many overseas markets. For a negotiated discount on prices, company B agrees to include the products of company A in its own marketing activities. Company A has little or no control in the overseas markets that are served, but can enjoy substantial extra business from this export source, albeit at a certain price.

Action: Identify companies within the industry, specified as exporters, from the *Kompass Directory*.

Manufacturer's export agent

The export agent markets and sells overseas on behalf of his UK principal. The agent provides specialist marketing skills, language skills, an intimate knowledge of local business practice and live buyer contacts. The agent is remunerated by commission and expenses. Usually the agent works for a number of principals each having complementary products. The products are sold in the manufacturer's name, so the principal retains control in the export market.

The manufacturer's export agent is to be distinguished from a local agent in the overseas market. Although their function in generating business for the manufacturer is the same, there is often much better communication between the manufacturer's export agent and his principal, than is established with overseas agents.

Action: For information contact:
The Institute of Export
64 Clifton Street
London WC2A 4HB
Tel. 01 247 9812
or:
Consultex Ltd
4 Ivor Close
Aldersley Road
Guildford
Surrey
GU1 2ET
Tel. 0483 578160

International contractors

Much business in the fields of construction, mining and oil exploration is carried out by British companies and consortia around the world. Some purchases are made locally to effect obvious savings. But a starting point for specialist suppliers of materials, personnel and professional skills is the UK offices of such companies. International tenders are published periodically in the financial and trade press.

Action: For information refer to the *Middle East Economic Digest* and *African Economic Digest* (both are published by Mead House, 21 John Street, London WC1N 2BP, tel. 01 404 5515).

Direct mail

Direct mail enjoys the advantages of privacy and selectivity.

It is an extremely cost-effective medium because export offers are made directly to the target-market segments. Wastage is kept to a minimum. Direct mail is a method of advertising in countries that have no real national TV or press media.

For client addresses additional to a company's own data base, there are two sources: (1) companies selling mail order lists and (2) companies providing a full mailing service. The names of both groups are found within Kompass directories. For most western trading markets it is possible to locate mail-order list companies based in the target market itself.

Action: The Post Office offers substantial introductory discounts for direct-mail campaigns. For information contact:
Direct Mail Department,
Post Office Headquarters,
Room 195,
33 Grosvenor Place
London SW1X 1EE, tel. 01 235 8000.

GETTING READY

Question **What preparations should precede the serious exporter's efforts to generate overseas business from within the UK?**

Sometimes the 'wrong' product sells despite the fact that it is 'wrong'. Getting the product right is no guarantee of success, but it is an essential step in exporting. The exporter should know – by finding out – how his product exactly matches the market needs.

When the products are sold through a third party, part of the workload is lifted. But if the would-be exporter makes the effort to learn about the market-place in which his goods are to be sold, more sales opportunities can be identified. Useful preliminary information is summarized below:

Checklist of important preparatory steps to exporting
Place tick in the appropriate box   YES NO

- Are the export objectives precise and quantifiable?   ☐   ☐

- Have all legal restrictions on market entry
  been identified?   ☐ ☐

- Do the products comply with local health
  requirements?   ☐ ☐

- Are all promotional/labelling constraints
  known?   ☐ ☐

- Are prices quoted in local currency?   ☐ ☐

- Is communication possible in the local
  language?   ☐ ☐

- Where appropriate, are prices quoted c.i.f.
  or d.d?   ☐ ☐

- Is the competition known?   ☐ ☐

- Are competitive pricing levels known?   ☐ ☐

- Are local business customs known?   ☐ ☐

If Yes, OK. If No, do something about it.

TRADING WITH NON-CURRENCY PAYMENT

Question **How is profitable export business organized for markets lacking convertible currency with which to make payment?**

When markets have no convertible currency with which to purchase goods and services, traditional exporting is made difficult. But the problem is not insoluble. Countertrade has been developed. It is a term covering export transactions in which an exporter accepts the importer's products in full or partial payment. In some countertrade transactions, partial cash payment is made. In others there is no cash payment at all.

There are four basic types of countertrade:

- barter
- compensation trading
- counterpurchase
- product buyback.

Barter   In barter there is a direct exchange of goods between the trading partners. No money changes hands. Barter transactions were commonplace in East–West trade in the years immediately following the Second World War. A typical example was Austrian shipment of wood against Hungarian shipment of food. Today genuine barter is less common. One problem is the reaching of agreement between the two parties on the agreed unit of exchange.

Compensation trading   With compensation trading the exporter accepts full or partial payment in kind from the trading partner. It is usually an exporter from an industrialized country supplying products to Eastern Europe or a Third World country. Figure 5.2 illustrates the mechanism of trading with full compensation. The importer exports goods from his market to a trading house or a third party in the Western world. The third party uses or sells the compensation goods and makes payment to the original exporter in convertible currency.

Figure 5.3 illustrates the mechanism of trading with partial

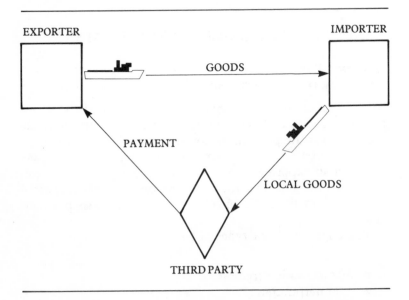

Figure 5.2 Mechanism of full-compensation trading

compensation. The Western exporter agrees to accept, say, 70 per cent payment in cash, with 30 per cent in local products. The importing country's goods are sold or used by a Western world third party, who makes appropriate payment to the original exporter.

Counterpurchase This is also known as parallel trade, reciprocal trade or counterdelivery. In counterpurchase an exporter commits himself, or a third party, to buying products from the importer equivalent to a certain percentage of his own deliveries. Figure 5.4 illustrates the mechanism of counterpurchase.

There are two chief differences between compensation trading and counterpurchase.

- In a counterpurchase deal the exporter gets full payment for his shipments immediately – or under credit terms. His own purchase obligations become due only when suitable products have been found and a contract signed. In compensation trading the exporter receives

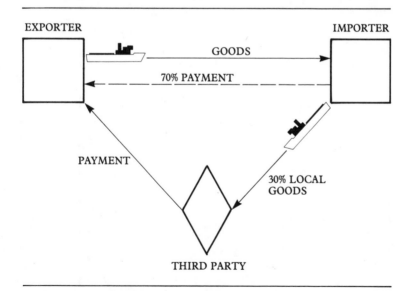

Figure 5.3   Mechanism of partial-compensation trading

payment from the third party, subject to the deliveries of the importer's goods.

● In counterpurchase deals two separate but linked contracts are signed: one contract for the sale of the Western products and a second contract in which the exporter undertakes to purchase products (often unspecified) from the importer, or the importer's associates, during a certain period of time. The time period is usually six to eighteen months. In compensation trading there is normally one contract signed by all parties.

Product buyback This type of deal is most commonly introduced in turnkey products. The exporter, usually a consortium, builds a plant in the importers' country. Frequently the transfer of technology is an integral part of the transaction. It is handed over when in full working order. Payment is then made in the products from the plant set up by the export consortium. Delivery of the goods is likely to be spread over a number of years.

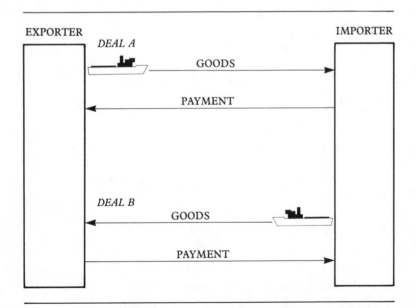

Figure 5.4 Mechanism of counterpurchase trading

SUMMARY

Question How important is it to visit overseas markets to take export orders?

Answer There is much export business that is available to would-be exporters from the home market. Both government and commercial organizations buy on behalf of overseas clients. Many overseas buying organizations maintain buying offices in the home market.

Question What organization is primarily concerned with export business originating from public sector clients overseas?

Answer Crown Agents is a government department which acts as a buying agent for overseas governments and local authorities.

Question What third-party trading organizations buy from sources in the home market, for overseas clients?

Answer There are various organizations that buy in the home market. They are confirming houses, export merchants and the export buying offices of overseas departmental store groups.

Question How is profitable export business organized for markets lacking convertible currency with which to make payment?

Answer Exporters seeking to trade with markets having no convertible currency get round the problem through countertrade transactions. Countertrade is made up of (1) barter, (2) compensation trading, (3) counterpurchase and (4) product buyback.

Question Through what circumstances are exporters able to meet overseas buyers in the home market?

Answer   Exporters meet overseas buyers in the UK through inward missions, at state trading offices and at home-market international exhibitions.

Question   **What opportunities exist in the UK to export as principals through third parties?**

Answer   Export business can be generated for companies through piggy-back marketing, where goods are carried by manufacturers of complementary products, using their established distribution channels. Additionally, manufacturer's export agents, international contractors and direct mail are sources of export business.

Question   **What preparations should precede the serious exporter's efforts to generate overseas business from within the UK?**

Answer   The exporter is beholden to find out how his product exactly matches the needs of customers in the marketplace in terms of legal limitations, health and safety factors, tariff obligations, composition, shape, packaging, price, and so on.

6 Appointing agents and distributors

Before reading this chapter, answer the following questions. The answers are worked through in the text. Question and answer are provided together at the end of the chapter as a summary.

QUESTIONS

What is the difference between an agent and a distributor?

What are the advantages and disadvantages of using an agent as compared to a distributor?

What does an agent require from the overseas principal?

What are the responsibilities of an agent towards his principal?

What are the criteria for agent selection?

How does an exporter find the names and addresses of agents and distributors to appoint overseas?

Chapter 6 synopsis

- Who does what overseas
- Weighing up the pros and cons
- The principal's obligations
- The principal's expectations
- How to choose
- Finding names and addresses

WHO DOES WHAT OVERSEAS

Question **What is the difference between an agent and a distributor?**

The roles of agent and distributor are frequently thought to be synonymous. But although the terms are often used loosely, in fact each has a specific function.

An agent is a person or company who sells goods and services on behalf of a principal. Remuneration is by way of commission achieved on sales made to customers. Goods are shipped by the principal directly to the customer. Payment for the goods supplied is made by the customer to the principal.

A distributor buys for his own account from a supplier and on-sells to the end user. The manufacturer or supplier does not usually know the identity of the final purchaser. The distributor is responsible for securing payment for goods sold to his own customers. Figure 6.1 illustrates how agents and distributors service a market.

WEIGHING UP THE PROS AND CONS

Question **What are the advantages and disadvantages of using an agent as compared to a distributor?**

In selling through agents and distributors, each method has advantages and disadvantages.

Selling through agents

Advantages

- Direct contract with all customers. If the services of an agent are discontinued, the relationship with established customers can be maintained.
- Full selling price is chargeable to all customers. It must be precisely agreed, whether commission is payable on the selling price, on the ex works price, on the f.o.b. price, or whatever. If it is payable on the CIF price, commission is being paid on the insurance and

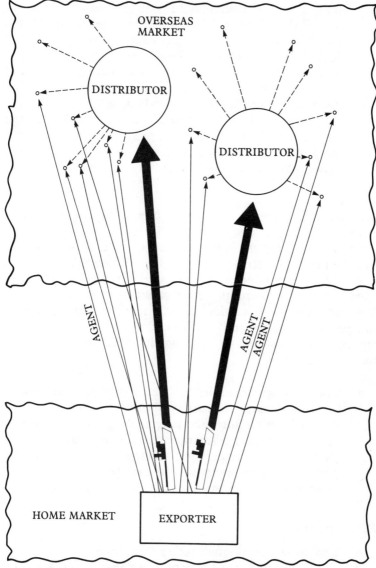

OPTION A Export with large orders to distributors supplying own customers
OPTION B Export at higher price directly to many small customers through agents

**Figure 6.1 How agents and distributors service an
export market**

freight charges. Commission rates vary with the industry. With fashion goods the rate may be 10 per cent.
In the steel industry it is 2 per cent or less.

- Selling costs are minimal. There are the initial setting-
up costs of screening applicants and visiting and inter-
viewing prospective agents. The agent must be supplied with samples of the product, either free or at
a substantial discount. There may be printing costs
for literature or instructions printed in the local market
language. After that, theoretically, orders taken by the
agent, working at his or her own expense, begin to
flow in.

Selling through agents overseas requires little initial investment. It is for this reason that it is seen as an easy pathway
for would-be exporters. But many times agents are appointed
and the principal then waits and waits for orders that never
come. The principal–agent relationship is rather like a marriage. As such both parties must work to achieve success.
It is necessary for the principal to visit the agent regularly
and provide support and motivation. Every principal visit
can be 'merchandised' by the agent to set up customer
appointments.

- There are opportunities for securing ongoing research
feedback from the market place. This requirement
should be built into every agency agreement. Every
agent must report regularly at weekly intervals on progress. News of impending changes in legislation, in
demand, in fashion trends, in new product usage, in
competitive action must be relayed to the principal.

Disadvantages

- Unit order size is small rather than large.
- Credit control management is necessary for a large
rather than a small number of customers.
- Additional packaging and transportation costs are incurred when there are many small consignments.
- The principal has no control over the sales effort given
to the product by the agent.

Selling through distributors

Advantages

- Orders are large rather than small.
- Savings in packaging, insurance and freight are achieved through container-sized shipments.
- The opportunities for bad debts are reduced by having a small rather than large number of buyers.
- Established distributors are often prepared to make prompt payment for their own deliveries in order to benefit from cash discounts.
- Distributors are in a position to provide pre-sales or after-sales service when this is a precondition of sale. They are also geared to maintaining spare-part stocks.

Disadvantages

- When bad debts do occur they can be substantial because of the volume of business transacted by distributors.
- Distributors demand a considerable discount on list prices because of the size of the orders placed. Margins vary with industries, but distributors work on a large return to compensate for their risks, investment and input. Distributors clear the goods through customs at the port or airport of entry, unpack, store and process for sale to their own customers.

THE PRINCIPAL'S OBLIGATIONS

Question What does an agent require from the overseas principal?

An agent lives by selling. From the sales, commissions are earned. Possession of an agency does not automatically provide the agent with money. From the agent's point of view there are good and bad agencies.

An agent wants:

A good product to sell Products that are new to a market and demand much groundwork before being accepted are unattractive to agents. The time that is necessary to gain consumer acceptance might be spent by the agent in selling products from other principals that have ready sales.

Reliable early deliveries Commission is not usually earned until the goods have been delivered. If the deliveries are extended, the agent must wait for commission payment.

Favourable commission terms Commission rates are frequently stable within an industry. The payment of larger than usual commissions diminishes profitability. Sometimes a higher than usual commission is offered to an agent for an introductory period, to launch a product that is new to a market. This is designed to compensate for the additional effort required. Careful consideration must be given to the psychological factor of demotivation when the commission rate reduces to that which is considered appropriate for normal sales.

When commission payments are to be made also requires careful consideration. Agents would naturally like payment as soon as the principal receives the orders, but this system is open to abuse. Fictitious orders can be sent that are subsequently cancelled. One equitable arrangement is payment at regular monthly intervals after customer payments have been received.

One situation where a higher than normal commission rate is payable is in a *del credere* agency. The agent agrees to take financial responsibility for the orders placed by his customers, covering the principal in the event of a default. Because of this commitment the agent makes an effort to ensure that there are no bad debts.

Favourable credit terms for customers The more attractive the deal for the customer, the easier it is for the agent to build up sales.

Advertising and promotional support The agent overseas is usually in a better position than the principal to advise on promotional input appropriate to the market. But specialist local advertising agencies are recommended whenever a significant advertising appropriation is available. When advertising campaigns are conducted in a number of overseas markets it is also wise to consider a single international agency able to integrate advertising on a global scale. Most agents ask the principal to bear the expense of promotion. Compromise, or support, is a matter of judgement for the principal.

Training in product knowledge and product usage Without doubt a sound knowledge of the product is a prerequisite of effective selling. When appropriate the agent should be invited to the factory for indoctrination and training. Any activity that reinforces a relationship between agent and principal is to be encouraged.

Competitive prices Non-price competition is a marketing activity – quality, reliability, innovation – that every exporter should explore and achieve. From the agent's point of view this is a complication. Agents, in general terms, believe that if the price is competitive (i.e. low), they can sell. If it is high, it is more difficult to sell. It is important that exporters' pricing policies start in the market-place and work backwards, so that the prices quoted are realistic and achieve maximum profitability.

THE PRINCIPAL'S EXPECTATIONS

Question **What are the responsibilities of the agent towards his principal?**

In the two-way relationship between agent and principal there are certain obligations that the agent must fulfil:

- Attract customers. The agent's task is to find new customers with whom to do business. The agent must be a self-starter, able to motivate and initiate without the prompting of the principal.
- Have a thorough product knowledge. Incomplete knowledge inhibits sales; it also diminishes the credibil-

ity of the principal's image and products in the market-
place.

- Acquire and maintain a thorough knowledge of the
  market. The agent should identify all the different segments into which the goods can be introduced.
- Know all the regulations. The agent must keep the
  principal informed of changes in respect of tariff regulations, exchange control, health, safety and legal
  requirements.
- Report regularly. The report should be sent weekly.
  Otherwise, when appropriate to negotiations, contact
  is made by phone or telex or fax.
- Maintain regular contact with customers. Prompt
  service, reliability and identification with customer
  problems are all ingredients of good business.
- Deal with complaints. This aspect of an agent's work
  is unproductive in that the time spent does not directly
  generate income. It is an integral part, none the less,
  of the agency function. Delays and problems of clearance at the docks and airports are examples. The principal also calls upon the agent to press for payment
  when settlement of accounts are not made.
- Identify appropriate training requirements. The
  agent's perception of training needs reinforces the principal's marketing approach to meet customer needs
  precisely.

In some markets, particularly the Middle East, agents are
called upon to carry stocks. Title of the goods does not pass
to the agent but remains with the principal. The agent provides storage and handling facilities on an expenses basis
and earns commission on the sales of goods.

A variation of this situation is when business is increased
through consignment trading. The judgement of the agent
and the principal is that there is the potential for transacting
additional business. The agent is not able to obtain firm
orders but is confident that when merchandise is quickly
available from stock it can be sold. The principal sends stocks
to the market-place. They are held, usually in a bonded warehouse so that no duties are payable until the goods are
required. The goods remain the property of the principal.

They are released on the instructions of the agent, when an appropriate order is passed. The agent is remunerated by commission on the sales, in accordance with agreed practice.

HOW TO CHOOSE

Question **What are the criteria for agent selection?**

In small markets the problems of selecting an agent who will generate good business are considerable. The agents with good track records are already committed. If the principal's products offer any kind of threat, the established agent may make an effort to secure the agency in order to 'sit' on it and prevent erosion of his existing business. There is usually no shortage of would-be agents. But how does one identify which inexperienced agent can rise to overcome the difficulties of customer resistance and disinterest? The checklist below provides a starting point for selection.

Other items should be added that are pertinent to specific industry requirements.

Checklist of criteria for agent selection

Place tick in the appropriate box   YES NO

- Are there live contacts in the market place?   ☐   ☐
- Is there a sound knowledge of the market?   ☐   ☐
- Is there evidence of a good business reputation?   ☐   ☐
- Is the agent financially sound?   ☐   ☐
- Has the agent provided details of other agencies held?   ☐   ☐
- Does a cross-check with the agent's other principals confirm that the information given is complete?   ☐   ☐
- Is there evidence of the agent's competence technically?   ☐   ☐

- Is there evidence that the agent can sell? □ □

- Does the agent have adequate language capability? □ □

- Is there evidence that the agent can cover
  the projected territory effectively? □ □

- Is the agent able to justify his projection of
  future business if the agency is granted? □ □

If the answer is Yes, OK. If No, probe to discover the extent
of shortcomings.

Would-be agents are invariably optimistic. They are certain
that good business will ensue. They are also determined to
wrest a sole-agency agreement from the new principal, for
as large a territory as can be secured. Exclusive rights are
a powerful marketing tool – when business goes well. Such
rights should not be granted lightly. Performance-related
safeguards can be introduced.

Territory demarcation is an important issue. It relates
geographically to a market. It also relates to specified products
or services supplied. How and when commission is paid on
business obtained from a territory has to be precisely stated.
Otherwise circumstances may arise when two agents claim
commission on the same business, each believing that their
claim is reasonable.

Example: Agent A sends in an order from a multiple outlet
customer, whose head office is within his territory. Some
of the goods are for delivery to an outlet sited within the
territory of the adjacent agent B. Agent B claims commission
on goods delivered within his territory. Agent A claims commission on goods delivered against his original order.

FINDING NAMES AND ADDRESSES

Question **How does an exporter find the names and addresses
of agents and distributors to appoint overseas?**

There are various channels through which an exporter finds
agents and distributors overseas. They are:

Personal contact Through experience of the trade, and from the variety of contacts and acquaintances built up in the course of business, suitable agents and distributors may be known.

Recommendations There is a difference between recommendations and personal contact. For example, the exporter goes to the overseas market. He asks existing or potential customers interested in the exporter's products to recommend an agent or distributor to handle the goods. The customer is often willing to do this because it provides a local contact. When the customer wants to call off from locally held stocks, a distributor is recommended. When the customer is prepared to undertake the import documentation and clearance, the name of an agent already serving the customer for another principal is provided.

Advertisement Advertisements inviting contact from agents and distributors are placed in the trade press of the local market and in appropriate local and national press. The trade association and the overseas posts of the British Overseas Trade Board can advise which papers are suitable. If the advertisement is translated into the local language, it is essential that the text is colloquially and grammatically correct. This criteria applies to all translation. An appropriate check is to use three stages:

1 Translate from English into the local language.
2 Have a third party translate the text back into English.
3 Compare the English translation with original text.

BOTB Export Representative Service This service is discussed in Chapter 4. For a fee the department provides a short list of businessmen in the market place. They will have been screened and will be specifically interested in working with the exporter's product or service.

Chambers of commerce Chambers will supply lists of names and addresses to anyone who asks, if it will promote the business of the members of the chamber. There is less co-operation if the objective is only to promote the business of the person or company making the enquiry. It is often expedient to take out membership of an overseas chamber of commerce – provided that research shows the potential for business in a particular market is good.

SUMMARY

Question   What is the difference between an agent and a distributor?

Answer   An agent sells on behalf of a principal and is remunerated by commission. A distributor buys for his own account selling on to his own customers.

Question   What are the advantages and disadvantages of using agents as compared to a distributor?

Answer   There are advantages and disadvantages in respect of each channel of distribution. Where a service element is an integral part of the sales function, a distributor is better equipped to provide such service.

Question   What does an agent require from the overseas principal?

Answer   An agent looks for competitively priced products that are easy to sell on favourable commission terms that have early delivery.

Question   What are the responsibilities of an agent towards his principal?

Answer   An agent's duties are to generate business for his principal by selling and by undertaking all the contingent activities that contribute to good business.

Question   What are the criteria for agent selection?

Answer When selecting an agent an exporter looks for evidence from performance, personality, resources and reputation that the agent has the motivation and capability to generate business.

Question How does an exporter find names and addresses of agents and distributors to appoint overseas?

Answer Names and addresses of agents and distributors are found through advertisements in the trade, local and national press, and by recommendation. Help is also available from the British Overseas Trade Board.

7 Beware agency contracts

Before reading this chapter, answer the following test questions. The answers are worked through in the text. Question and answer are provided together at the end of the chapter as a summary.

QUESTIONS

How important is a formal contract with overseas agents and distributors?

What should an agency agreement cover?

How important is it for the agency agreement to incorporate reference to every possible eventuality?

What differences, if any, are there between an agency agreement and an agreement with a distributor?

What argument supports the view that a short contractual agreement with distributors based on mutual understanding and trust is preferable to a comprehensive, precisely detailed document?

Is an exporter clear of obligation to an agent once the term of a concluded agreement is reached?

Chapter 7 synopsis

- The value of a legal document
- Points of agreement
- How comprehensive must an agreement be?
- Dealing with agents and distributors
- A place for mutual trust
- Interpretation according to English law

THE VALUE OF A LEGAL DOCUMENT

Question How important is a formal contract with overseas agents and distributors?

Though the terms are often used indiscriminately, there is in law a clear distinction between the activities and functions of overseas agents and distributors. Distributors carrying stocks are often referred to as agents, the real distinction being that they are not the manufacturers.

Business can be transacted without any formal agreement. As long as both parties are in accord, business can commence and grow. There are no limitations as long as there is harmony. Problems arise when there is a dispute, and there are many opportunities for dispute in the export trade. For example, an agent passes an order to his UK principal for Christmas tree decorations. The order is accepted and despatched within the quoted delivery time. The goods are delayed at the docks due to industrial action until after Christmas. The customer refuses to take up and pay for the goods. The agent claims commission due on the order. The manufacturer is reluctant to pay commission. Not only has he lost business, there are also expenses to be borne in retrieving the rejected goods, and the resale value of the goods is reduced because of their seasonal nature.

In fact, the exporter may have a legitimate claim against the carriers and may be able to recoup the financial loss, including the commission payment due. The exporter may also have credit insurance cover for most of the loss, through the Exports Credits Guarantee scheme. There is another option. With regard to the agent, the exporter may decide to pay out the commission, whether or not the goods or their value are recovered.

When a contract is concluded between a principal and his agent or distributor, it should be constructed to resolve all matters of dispute likely to arise. In the example given, recourse to a formal agency agreement settles the problem, provided that the situation has been covered.

The absence of a contract is not necessarily a safeguard for the exporter. Performance can provide evidence that a contract was the intention between two parties, whether or not an actual document is signed and witnessed.

POINTS OF AGREEMENT

Question   **What should an agency agreement cover?**

A number of important factors must be taken into consideration when making arrangements between the exporter and an agent overseas. When an agency contract is drawn up, the following aspects should be discussed by both parties and incorporated in the agreement:

- A statement of the parties to the agreement.
- The purpose of the agreement. One party agrees to appoint the other as agent. The other agrees to act as agent, subject to the terms and conditions stated.
- The territory. Geographically the territory may be an entire country (e.g. South Africa). It may be a region of a country (e.g. northern Italy, comprising all towns and land north of Florence). Or it may be bounded by political borders (e.g. the EEC).
- The product range. Sometimes a manufacturer employs more than one agent in the same territory, selling different items produced within the organization. Usually the products are differentiated by value added; for example, a textile manufacturer may sell in the same territory piece goods and made-up garments from those piece goods.
- The principal's discretion to accept orders. The agent's duty is to obtain orders but not to enter into binding

contracts on the principal overseas. The principal confirms all orders placed. This is a safeguard against orders being placed that cannot be executed for reasons of inadequate production capacity or time limitation.

- Commission. It must be stated on what basis the commission is to be paid; for example, how much commission is payable and whether it is calculated on an ex works, f.o.b., c.i.f. or other basis. The frequency of payment is also to be given; for example, after each order is executed, or after payment is received, or monthly, or quarterly. Provision is usually made for commission to be paid on all business emanating from an agent's territory, with the exception of house accounts. This means that commission is payable on orders executed, whether the customer gives the order to the agent or makes direct contact with the exporter.

- House accounts. There are often existing clients in a territory before the agent is appointed. Because of strong personal relationships that exist between the principal and such clients, they are nominated as falling outside the agent's sphere of activity. No commission is payable for goods delivered to such clients, notwithstanding arrangements for commission payable on all direct and indirect business.

- Consignment goods. The terms are given under which consignment deliveries are made; that is, how goods are to be disposed of on termination of the agreement.

- Term of agency agreement. The period for which the agreement is binding must be stated as well as the length of notice prior to termination by either party. Termination is to be notified formally in writing.

- Duties of the principal. The main duties of the principal are
  - to pay the agent commissions due
  - to pay expenses and provide an indemnity if loss is suffered. The principal's right to deal with other agents or to make sales to the territory other than through the agent is to be clearly defined.

- Duties of an agent. The main duties of the agent are:
  - to use reasonable diligence
  - to disclose all material facts to the principal

- not to accept bribes or make secret profits
- not to divulge confidential information
- to account to the principal.

- Assignment. The benefits and obligations of the agency contract may not be assigned without the joint agreement of both parties.
- Force majeure. The principal is to be free from responsibility for late delivery if due to *force majeure*. The principal shall advise the agent promptly and, where necessary, supply a certificate.

HOW COMPREHENSIVE MUST AN AGREEMENT BE?

Question   How important is it for the agency agreement to incorporate reference to every possible eventuality?

An agreement designed to protect both parties against every conceivable principal–agency conflict would be a very long document. Most companies develop a wide range of contracts to suit different situations in different markets. The starting point is a basic contract incorporating items that are common to every contract.

Hanovia Ltd are a UK company manufacturing water purification systems equipment. They have given permission for their basic agency agreement form to be published. It is their starting point for the agreements in the many markets to which they export.

Basic agency agreement for Hanovia Ltd

This AGENCY AGREEMENT is being entered into this by and between HANOVIA LIMITED, 145 Farnham Road, Slough, Berkshire, England, hereinafter called the 'PRINCIPALS', of the first part,

and

hereinafter called the 'AGENTS', of the second part,

AND WITNESSETH AS FOLLOWS:

1. The PRINCIPALS appoint the AGENTS as the sole representative and agent in
(hereinafter referred to as the 'TERRITORY') to exclusively sell and distribute the products made by the PRINCIPALS which are generally:

Industrial water disinfection systems

Domestic water disinfection systems

trademarked as HANOVIA (hereinafter referred to as the 'PRODUCTS') and manufactured in the United Kingdom from predominantly British materials.

2. This Agreement is in force for a first period of two (2) years from the above date this Agreement was entered into. The Agreement shall thereafter be automatically renewed for a period of one year unless the Agreement is terminated in writing at least ninety (90) days before the renewal date.

3. The AGENTS undertake to make the HANOVIA PRODUCTS known in the TERRITORY and to use their best endeavours to maximise sales of the PRODUCTS.

4. The AGENTS undertake not to promote or sell any products which compete directly with the products during the validity of this agreement.

5. The PRINCIPALS undertake to provide the AGENTS with reasonable quantities of catalogues, leaflets, price lists and other sales promotion and advertising materials.

6. The PRINCIPALS undertake to keep the AGENTS informed about changes in range and price and technical specifications and to provide copies of all correspondence with the TERRITORY.

7. Commission will be paid to the AGENTS at the rate of
per cent (%) on the ex works value of direct sales to the TERRITORY at the full list price ruling at that time and will become payable only when payment is received by the PRINCIPALS. Where the price is reduced by joint

negotiation between the PRINCIPALS AND AGENTS then the first per cent reduction in price will be deducted from the AGENTS COMMISSION and further reductions will on agreement be shared equally between the PRINCIPALS and the AGENTS.

8. In case that the PRINCIPALS are contacted or approached by any third party knowingly for the supply to the TERRITORY, the PRINCIPALS agree to seek approval of the exclusive AGENTS prior to supply, such approval not to be unreasonably withheld.

   Commission for the AGENTS in such instances shall be negotiated in each case but shall be a minimum of per cent (%) of the PRINCIPALS' net realized ex works value of the sale.

9. Any dispute that might arise on the interpretation and/or conflict over this Agreement, will be governed by the Commercial Laws of the United Kingdom.

IN WITNESS WHEREOF, the Parties hereinto set their signature to the date specified beforehand.

FOR & ON BEHALF OF
HANOVIA LIMITED

FOR & ON BEHALF OF

(PRINCIPALS)

(AGENTS)

Particular items of note are:

Item 2 The agreement is in force for an initial period of two years, and automatically renewed in yearly periods unless specifically cancelled.

Item 3 Commission is payable on ex works values of goods.

Item 9 Any dispute arising in respect of the agreement is governed by the commercial laws of the UK. However, notwithstanding what is agreed between the two parties, in some countries the law of the agent's country *must* apply.

DEALING WITH AGENTS AND DISTRIBUTORS

Question What differences, if any, are there between an agency agreement and an agreement with a distributor.

The legal position of a sole distributor is very different from that of an agent, notwithstanding that they both operate in an exclusive territory. A distributor buys goods from the principal and resells them in his territory. The distributor or importer is not part of the distribution channel that the principal has with a third party in the export market. The distributor is the exporter's sole contracting party in the export market. When the distributor resells, he enters into new contracts of sale with the customers in his territory – be they wholesalers, retailers or the public.

From a legal point of view, it is therefore essential that the exporter's agreement with the distributor makes it clear that *the distributor is not entitled to act for, on behalf of, or in the name of, the principal.* If the end user has cause to make a claim, it is only against the distributor. The distributor in turn must then make claim on the exporter.

In a distribution agreement the following points should be covered:

- Trial period. Before the contract is closed a probationary period allows distributor performance to be evaluated.
- Patents, brand names, trade marks. Careful attention is necessary for the protection of rights. In respect of brand names, care is essential to ensure that local pronunciation or meaning has no adverse effect on promotion; for example, an American company marketing Pet milk experienced difficulties introducing its products into French speaking countries. In French the word means, amongst other things, 'to break wind'.
- Advertising costs and promotional material. The respective contribution between parties for advertising and promotion should be clearly defined.
- Price escalation clause. A mechanism is appropriate by which the principal has the right to increase prices.
- Termination clause. The termination clause is of vital

importance. It must say precisely how the contract is either automatically terminated or terminated by notice. It must further set out details for the disposal of stocks, samples, catalogues, advertising material or equipment that are in the possession of the distributor.

A PLACE FOR MUTUAL TRUST

Question What argument supports the view that a short contractual agreement with distributors based on mutual understanding and trust is preferable to a comprehensive, precisely detailed document?

When an exporter, working with his legal advisers, prepares a distributor contract, he seeks to cover every eventuality. Every clause, while striving for a balance between the two parties, works primarily for the interests of the exporter. This is natural and understandable. But the importer/distributor also works with legal advisers. There are similar objectives orientated towards the distributor's interests. The outcome, when accord is reached, can be a long, comprehensive document.

When a dispute does occur reference is made to the distributor contract simply because it has been formulated – and because it is there. There is a tendency even for minor disputes to be dealt with in this way. Opportunities for ad hoc resolution of disputes are restricted because precedents have been set.

L.G. Harris and Co. Ltd, Bromsgrove, UK are multinational brush manufacturers. They export a substantial volume of products worldwide. One of the countries with which the company does business is the Sultanate of Oman. In certain countries of the Gulf, of which Oman is one, an agent/distributor needs a certified and registered agreement to be permitted to tender for government contracts. Harris Ltd negotiated with an agent/distributor to represent them in the Sultanate of Oman. The agency sent to their principals an eight-page foolscap-size draft contract for signature. Some of the clauses in the proposed contract are reproduced below. They are selected to show how the agent approaches the relationship with benefits to the agent foremost.

Extracts from proposed Shanfari–L.G. Harris Agreement

3. Term of Appointment

The appointment of the distributor shall commence with effect from the 1st January 1985 and shall (unless previously determined under the provisions hereinafter contained) remain in force unless terminated by either party giving to the other not less than six (6) calendar months' notice in writing to that effect expiring on or at any time after the 31st December 1985.

5(b) All invoices will be due and payable 120 days after clearance from an Oman port or as otherwise agreed between the supplier and distributor in writing.

6(d) It is agreed that the distributor may fulfil an urgent order (for a valued customer) by purchase other than from the supplier if the latter cannot supply and provided the distributor obtains his authority beforehand.

7. Suppliers Covenants

The supplier hereby undertakes that during the continuance of this agreement:

(c) It will send to the territory a representative with technical or specialized knowledge of the products, and the industry in which they are used, to call on all customers.

The frequency of these visits are to be agreed between the supplier and the distributor but not to be less than every three months.

(d) The supplier shall upon shipment, or within five (5) working days of shipment, send a notice of shipment to the distributor by telex or telegraph, and the confirmation thereof by air letter. The notification shall contain the following information:

1 Name of the vessel
2 Date of sailing
3 Port of Destination
4 Description of goods and shipping marks
5 Contract number
6 Bill of lading number

7 Total number of packages
8 Gross weight
9 Total quantity of merchandise

The Supplier shall bear all damages such as demurrage incurred by the distributor as a result of late notification as required above.

11. Arrangements pursuant to Termination

(b) On termination however caused:

(ii) the supplier will at the distributor's sole discretion re-purchase at the net prices paid by the distributor any or all of the products remaining in the distributor's stock.

14. Governing Law, Arbitration and Calendar

(a) This agreement shall be construed in accordance with and governed by English law except to the extent that English law shall be in conflict with the law for the time being in force in the territory when the provisions of the law for the time being in force in the territory will apply, and in any dispute or difference between the parties hereunder (which cannot be resolved by amicable agreement between the parties) will be referred to arbitration by the Committee for the Settlement of Commercial Disputes in Muscat, Oman or to any court or tribunal established in succession thereto in accordance with the provisions of the Commercial Agencies Law.

(b) All dates and periods of time referred to in this agreement will be constructed in accordance with the Gregorian calendar.

L.G. Harris Ltd, preferring to conduct their export business on the basis of mutual understanding, reached formal agreement with a short document. It is reproduced with permission below.

Agency agreement for L.G. Harris Ltd

AGENCY AGREEMENT between L.G. Harris and Co.

Ltd., Stoke Prior, Bromsgrove, Worcestershire, U.K. (herein-after called 'The Principal') and Shanfari Trading and Con-tracting Co. L.L.C., C.R. No. 655, P.O. Box 783, Muscat, Sultanate of Oman (hereinafter called 'The Agent').

1. The Principal appoints the Agent to be the exclusive importer and distributor in the Sultanate of Oman (hereinafter called 'The Territory') for the importation and distribution of the full range of products manufactured by the Principal.

2. The Agent will use his best endeavours to safeguard and promote the interests of the Principals and to obtain the widest distribution and highest value turnover within the Territory.

3. The Principal agrees to acknowledge all orders received from the Agent in writing and to execute these orders as required.

4. If in any circumstances the Principal stops production of any particular type of machine or tool, then he will be respon-sible for reimbursement of the value of the spare parts held in the agents stock at that time.

5. The Principal agrees not to deliver mechandise or to provide quotations to third parties within the Territory without the prior authorisation of the Agent. When any such deliveries to third parties are executed on the request of the Agent, the Agent will specify the terms of payment to be utilized in the transaction and will guarantee payment to the Principal for merchandise supplied.

6. This Agreement is valid for two years commencing on the 1st February, 1986. It can be cancelled by either party giving notice of termination of a minimum of six months before the end of this period.

7. In the case of termination by the Principals, the Principal will arrange to transfer any stocks of merchandise held by the Agent to such other customers or agents as may be appointed for the Territory. In the case of termination by the Agents, the Agent will afford every assistance to the Princi-pal in finding an alternative agent to take over the distribution.

INTERPRETATION ACCORDING TO ENGLISH LAW

Question Is an exporter clear of obligation to an agent once the term of a concluded agreement is reached?

Some foreign laws provide considerable protection for the independent agent. In particular, the agent is entitled to claim compensation, after termination of the agency, for goodwill built up that continues to accrue to the principal. Claims for compensation are admitted in Germany, France, Italy, Switzerland and Austria.

An approach to avoid such claims is to make sure that the agency agreement is governed by English law. Exporters are advised to obtain from the commercial office of the embassy of the country to which they are exporting, notice of all laws pertaining to agency agreements.

In the event that the law of the country must be applied in interpretation of all agreements, the insertion of a clause to the effect that the agreement is to be governed by English law, is of no avail.

SUMMARY

Question How important is a formal contract with overseas agents and distributors?

Answer A contract is important. It attempts to safeguard both sides by setting out points of prior agreement. Provided that reference to any disputes subsequently arising is embodied in the contract, there is a mechanism for resolving that dispute.

Question What should an agency agreement cover?

Answer There are a number of important considerations to be included in an agreement. They are reflected in the following headings: a statement of the parties to the agreement;

the territory; the product range; the principal's discretion to accept orders; commission; house accounts; consignment goods; terms of agency agreement; duties of the principal; duties of the agent; assignment; *force majeure*.

Question How important is it for the agency agreement to incorporate reference to every possible eventuality?

Answer A document covering every eventuality is going to be a very long document. Some companies make use of a standard form of contract that is adapted to the specific obligations and demands of the different export markets.

Question What differences, if any, are there between an agency agreement and an agreement with a distributor?

Answer From a legal point of view the distributor agreement must make it clear that the distributor is not entitled to act for, on behalf of, or in the name of, the principal. This situation pertains, notwithstanding that both the agent and the distributor may act in exclusive territories.

Question What argument supports the view that a short contractual agreement with distributors based on mutual understanding and trust is preferable to a comprehensive, precisely detailed document?

Answer When there is a particularly comprehensive distributor agreement there is a tendency for even minor disputes to be resolved strictly in accordance with the agreement. Another option is to have a short basic document covering essential points of accord. Both parties endeavour to conduct their relationship on the basis of mutual understanding and trust.

Question Is an exporter clear of obligation to an agent once the term of a concluded agreement is reached?

Answer In some overseas markets there is considerable protection for the agent. If procedure in the event of termination is specified, and the contract is to be interpreted in accordance with English law, no problems should arise. A proviso is that there is compliance with the appropriate procedure. If agreements must be interpreted in accordance with the laws of the overseas country, the particular agreement terms may be overruled and a form of compensation payable.

8 Getting regular business from agents and distributors

Before reading the chapter, answer the following test questions. The answers are worked through in the text. Question and answer are provided together at the end of the chapter as a summary.

QUESTIONS

How much training should be offered to new agents and distributors?

What are the chief functions of the principal visit?

What preparations should be made for a principal visit to an agent overseas?

What is the best way of obtaining regular market research feedback from an overseas agent?

When is investment in local advertising and promotion expedient for an export market?

What factors should an exporter consider when advertising overseas?

How does an exporter obtain regular feedback on performance from appointed agents and distributors?

> *Chapter 8 synopsis*
>
> - Training for performance
> - The principal visit
> - Visit preparation
> - Ongoing research from the market-place
> - Using advertising and promotion
> - An advertising structure
> - Monitoring performance overseas

TRAINING FOR PERFORMANCE

Question **How much training should be offered to new agents and distributors?**

Training is important for agents and for distributors. But there is an essential distinction. When a distributor buys goods from an overseas supplier he is committed to paying for those goods. If he does not sell the stocks his business suffers. There is strong motivation for the distributor to become good at selling. If new techniques are to be learnt for specific products, the distributor is eager to learn. It is different with an agent. If products do not sell easily, the agent gives up. He concentrates his efforts on the merchandise of other principals, where sales resistance is more easily overcome.

When an agent is appointed, support is therefore essential. But the agent is likely to have some selling skills, otherwise he or she could not survive as an agent. A training audit is helpful to identify the areas where training is appropriate. Figure 8.1 illustrates the training audit grid. It covers the different activities of an agent's work cycle:

- prospecting for business
- the sales presentation
- negotiating skills
- getting repeat business
- planning.

Each section is subdivided into component activities. The

agent should be questioned on each activity to identify competence and skill. A mark from 1 (weak) to 7 (strong) is given. This highlights areas where particular training is needed.

The training audit prompt questions below provide guidelines for the exporter's questions. In some markets where facilities are primitive, the questions relating to phone and postal activities are not relevant.

Training audit prompt questions

Prospecting

By phone:

- Do you use the phone to sell?
- Do you use the phone to make appointments?
- Do you use the phone to advise if you are late for an appointment?
- How do you eliminate calls having little chances of success?
- Do you use a script for the phone calls?
- What do you do when the customer says 'No'?
- When the call is not succeeding how do you pave the way for future contact?
- Do you maintain careful records of all prospecting calls?

By letter:

- Do you have the resources to prospect by letter?
- Do you have an effective format for a prospecting letter?
- Do you confirm business appointments by letter?
- Is your correspondence with customers business-like and efficient?

By cold canvass:

- How frequently do you make cold calls?
- Is block canvassing likely to generate good business?
- What target number of cold calls per customer visit is practical?

Agent _____ Market _____ Date _____ Controller _____

	Weak 1	2	3	4	5	6	Strong 7
PROSPECTING SKILL							
by 'phone							
letter							
cold canvass							
PRESENTATIONAL SKILL							
Visual aids							
Qualifying customer needs							
Passing benefit messages							
Overcoming·customer objections							
Closing							
Increasing order size							
NEGOTIATING SKILL							
Preparation							
Tactics							
Ability to create variables							
Bargaining skills							
GETTING REPEAT BUSINESS							
Post-delivery visit							
Regular visit							
By telephone							
By referrals							
PLANNING							
Call cycle							
Personal time management							
Report writing							

Use the training audit prompt questions (pp.127-132) to probe agent's performance and abilities. Evaluate performance on a scale from 1 to 7. Enter mark by ticking appropriate column.

Figure 8.1 Training audit grid

- Have you evolved an effective introductory gambit for the cold call?
- Do you maintain records of all cold calls made?

Sales presentation

Samples/visual aids:

- What samples/visual aids do you normally use?
- How can visual aids reinforce your sales presentation?
- At what stage of the presentation should samples/visual aids be introduced?

Qualifying customer needs:

- What questions identify customer interest?
- What questions pinpoint customer needs?

Product benefit messages:

- What contribution do benefit messages make to winning sales?
- What techniques are useful in passing benefit messages?

Overcoming customer objections:

- How do you overcome a customer's 'No'?
- What do you do when a customer says, 'I will think about it'?
- How do you identify whether a customer's objection is the real objection?
- What important rule or rules apply when countering a customer's objections?

Closing:

- How many closing techniques do you know?
- How many closes do you use?
- How often do you use trial closes?
- What do you do when the customer says 'No'?

Increasing the customer's order size:

- When should one attempt to increase the order size?
- How is the order size increased?

- How frequently should pressure be applied to the customer to give bigger orders?

Negotiating skills

Preparation:

- What is the difference between negotiating and selling?
- How does one prepare for negotiations?
- What do you understand by the three negotiating positions?
  - Must achieve or deadlock
  - Intend to achieve
  - Would like to achieve

Ability to create variables:

- What is the value of a variable in negotiation?
- What can be termed variables in respect of the products we are discussing?

Tactics:

- What different tactics are effective in negotiation?
- How can you create time to think in a negotiation when the other side takes you by surprise?

Bargaining skills:

- What questions should always be asked before granting a concession?
- What do you consider to be the most important rules of bargaining?
- What is the effect of the other side linking all their issues together?

Getting repeat business

Post-delivery visit:

- What are the objectives of calling on a customer after delivery is made?
- What is an appropriate format of the post-delivery visit?

Regular visit:

- How frequently should regular visits be made to customers?
- Is it feasible to sell the idea of a phone call instead of a visit, to save the customer time?
- What is the approach you adopt on a regular call to a customer?
- What innovations are likely to increase the volume of business obtained?

Telephone call:

- Is it possible to take repeat business by phone?
- Should the phone be used to make an appointment before calling for repeat business?
- Has a script been developed to secure repeat business by phone?

Referrals:

- Have you ever asked customers to recommend other buyers?
- When is the best time to ask for a referral?
- Have you ever asked a buyer to introduce you to another buyer?
- What form of incentive would motivate a buyer to recommend another buyer?

Planning

Call cycle:

- Taking into account your other commitments, how frequently would our customers be called on?
- What proportion of business is likely to come from what proportion of customers? That is, would 80 per cent of orders come from 20 per cent of the customers?
- How frequently do you call on the most important customer?
- How much time do you consider is necessary to build up a satisfactory customer base?

Personal time management:

- Do you achieve everything that you set out to do?
- Do you plan your day?
- Would you like help in improving the management of personal time?

Report writing:

- When do you write up notes on performance?
- What records do you keep?
- What is the most common cause of interruption to your report writing programme?
- What is your understanding of the reason why we insist on receiving regular reports from you?

THE PRINCIPAL VISIT

Question **What are the chief functions of the principal visit?**

When a principal visits his agent in the field there is a marketing opportunity to generate business. There are a number of reasons why a visit is so important:

Administration There is an opportunity to resolve administrative problems that arise through constraints on communication.

Application While the principal is present the agent is devoting his full attention and energy to promoting the company products.

Motivation The principal's interest and support in resolving the agent's problems of generating business reinforces the principal–agent relationship. The stronger the bonds that are established, the greater is the motivational momentum that helps the agent sell when the principal is away.

Refresher training Opportunities for creating business are greatest when the product or service is presented to the client in the most effective way. The principal is able to monitor the strengths and weaknesses of the agent's selling style.

Generating business The principal in the home market may be a one-man business operating from an upstairs bedroom.

Or the principal may be the chief executive of a public company. In the export market the principal is the respected authority behind the goods or services that are offered. Psychologically, customers prefer to deal with the highest authority. It enhances their own self-image. It is also an opportunity for decision-making. Ad hoc decisions can lead to business contracts unobtainable by an agent distanced by telex communication from his principal.

In many markets, particularly Japan and the Middle East, the prospects for establishing initial business are remote without the presence of the principal. It is important that the status of the export company representative is reflected as of the highest seniority.

In some markets, for example Saudi Arabia, legislation permits the import of foreign merchandise only through the medium of a local agent, who is a national of the country. Notwithstanding, the presence of senior management of the export company throughout the preliminary negotiations is essential.

VISIT PREPARATION

Question **What preparations should be made for a principal visit to an agent overseas?**

The leverage of a principal visit in generating export business is a fact. The potential is diluted if the opportunities contingent upon a visit are not exploited to the full. The section below covers preparations for a full principal/agent visit schedule.

Principal/agent visit checklist

Place tick in appropriate box   YES NO

- Arrange appointments with existing customers.   ☐ ☐
- Set up appointments to visit potential customers.   ☐ ☐
- Monitor credit status of potential customers;

monitor credit status of those customers
defaulting on credit payment terms.   □   □
- Confirm all appointments by telex or letter.   □   □
- Send literature samples to potential
  customers.   □   □
- Release details of new products to be
  launched, to trade press and local or national
  press.   □   □
- Prepare the logistical details to consider the
  option of increasing business through
  consignment trading.   □   □
- Consider the potential for increased business, through a local advertising and promotional campaign.   □   □
- Evaluate the potential for business through
  establishing a marketing office/break bulk
  depot in conjunction with the agent.   □   □
- Evaluate, with the agent, the success of the
  agent's sales performance.   □   □

If Yes, OK. If No, do something about it.

ONGOING RESEARCH FROM THE MARKET-PLACE

Question **What is the best way of obtaining regular market research feedback from an overseas agent?**

Control in the market-place is the pathway to good business. Control comes from close familiarity with the forces that operate within the market. Ideally a market launch is not made until preliminary researches have indicated that opportunities for success are present. But export initiatives do not always wait until all signs are propitious. It is therefore important that agents are pressed to give continuous feedback. Information so gained can reinforce the preliminary data base of information, assembled before market entry.

The following section illustrates the kind of questionnire that should be completed by the agent every six months:

Agent's market research questionnaire

Product/Service

- What competing brands take business away?
- What is the format/composition/quality of the products with the leading market share?
- What is the potential size of the market for the next year?
- What are the present product or service deficiencies?
- What stage in the product life-cycle is the product at?
- What is the lead delivery time for competitive products to the retail outlets?

Price

- What are the competitive price ranges?
- What non-price benefits do similar products offer?
- What price increases have there been in the last six months?
- Would price lining (i.e. holding the price and reducing the quantity/quality) be preferable to a price increase?
- What change in business is likely to result from a price increase of 5 per cent, of 10 per cent, of 15 per cent, of 20 per cent, of 25 per cent, of 33 per cent, of 50 per cent?

Promotion

- What point-of-sale promotion is adopted by the competition?
- What percentage increase in price would be justified by media advertising?
- What significant changes in product promotion have taken place in the last six months?
- In what directories, yearbooks or buyer's guides should the product name appear?
- At what exhibitions should the product be promoted?
- How do our guarantees/warranties compare with those of the competition?
- What is the customer's perception of the quality of our product?

- In which journals, papers, magazines and trade press should we seek to obtain editorial publicity?

Distribution

- Which are the largest groups of customers to whom we are selling?
- Which significant customer groups have not yet bought our products?
- Are there any groups of customers who might use our products for a different purpose from that normally adopted?
- What complementary products or services are carried by competitive agents?

USING ADVERTISING AND PROMOTION

Question **When is investment in local advertising and promotion expedient for an export market?**

An important ingredient of success in an export market is personal selling. The return from expenditure on the support functions of promotion and advertising varies, depending on the nature of the product and the type of distribution channel. But advertising and promotion are an investment. The return is reflected in one or more of a number of ways:

- market entry
- consumer education
- product acceptance
- neutralizing competitor strategies
- increased volume of sales
- increased number of outlets.

Different forms of advertising and promotion are appropriate to industrial products and to consumer goods.

With fast-moving consumer goods the full benefit of an advertising campaign is unlikely to be gained when export business is taken through the services of agents. An agent cannot devote his or her full time to selling, because of commitments to other principals. Often back-up stocks are not available, which dilutes or neutralizes the impact of advertising. The situation is different when there are distributors who do carry stocks. Carefully planned campaigns in magazines, the press, on television, on radio and by poster all contribute to increased business.

For consumer goods, promotion supports agents' and distributors' efforts in three ways:

- Point of sale material. The material must be designed to complement local taste and culture. Messages must be in the local language.
- In-store promotion and demonstration. The BOTB offers advice and support.
- Exhibitions.

With industrial products, advertising campaigns are directed in a direction different from that for consumer goods. They take the form of listed and display entries in trade directories and the trade press, as opposed to being aimed at the consumer. The purpose is twofold:

- to give credibility to the representative in the market-place
- to invite technical interest from specialist buyers.

Exhibitions are of particular importance in promotion. Opportunities are provided for the display and demonstration of equipment not always available to agents and distributors.

AN ADVERTISING STRUCTURE

Question What factors should an exporter consider when advertising overseas?

Advertising and promotion, together, make up an important variable of the marketing mix. They are under the control of the exporter. As such there should be a budget allocation. Whether the appropriation is large or small, advertising is a planned activity, working to achieve set objectives. When the appropriation is large, it is unwise not to consider the advice of specialist advertising agencies having local experience. Certainly the advice of the importer or distributor

is sought too.   Advertising decisions are made under a
number of headings, given below:

The advertising message

- standardization
- cultural limits
- social constraints
- legal restrictions
- translation.

Media selection

- target audience statistics
- literacy
- media availability
- regionalization
- overspill
- print quality
- legal constraints.

Agency selection

- market coverage
- creativity
- cost.

MONITORING PERFORMANCE OVERSEAS

Question How does an exporter obtain regular feedback on performance from appointed agents and distributors?

The 'marriage' of the exporter to the new agent is always
exciting. There is the potential of new business. But to plead
the case for appointment as agent, optimism reinforces
realism in assessment of likely business. When the appointment is concluded, the exporter moves on to the next market
or returns to home base. He then waits for news of success.
Sometimes he waits and waits. In other situations the orders
roll in.

It is important for the exporter to know the situation in
the overseas market. This is achieved by regular feedback.

A frequent problem is to motivate the agent to report regularly, particularly through the times when business is slow.

At the outset, reporting procedures should be clearly defined. Figure 8.2 shows a reporting sheet designed to be completed and posted weekly. While agents initially consent to meet the agreed demands of their new principals, the situation changes when they are alone in their territory and business conditions are adverse. Exporters must highlight the importance of the weekly report. It is necessary that agents see their principals as successful through efficient management and leadership.

SUMMARY

Question How much training should be offered to new agents and distributors?

Answer In addition to product knowledge training, selling skills should be reinforced. Areas of weakness are identified using a training audit grid.

Question What are the chief functions of the principal visit?

Answer The important functions of the principal visit are: (1) administration, (2) work application, (3) motivation, (4) refresher training and (5) generating business.

Question What preparations should be made for a principal visit to an agent overseas?

Answer Prior to appointments are to be made and confirmed with existing and new customers, and with the embassy commercial office before a principal visit.

Question What is the best way of obtaining regular market research feedback from an overseas agent?

Agent _____

Territory _____

Week No.	Date	Customer contact		Business Taken	ACTION
		Old	New		
1					
			Total	£	
2					

Figure 8.2 Agent's weekly report form

Answer The task of the agent should be simplified by providing a market research questionnaire to be completed every six months.

Question What form of local advertising and promotion are expedient for an export market?

Answer The investment in overseas advertising and promotion varies depending on the distribution channel and depending on whether the product is in the category of fast moving consumer goods (FMCG) or industrial product.

Question What factors should an exporter consider when advertising overseas?

Answer Advertising decisions are made under a number of headings: (1) the advertising message, (2) media selection and (3) agency selection.

Question How does an exporter obtain regular feedback on performance from appointed agents and distributors?

Answer The agent's task must be simplified by means of a pre-printed report form, to be completed and sent to the exporter weekly.

9 Exporting with minimal investment

Before reading the chapter, answer the following test questions. The answers are worked through in the text. Question and answer are provided together at the end of the chapter as a summary.

QUESTIONS

What is a licensing agreement?

What marketing conditions particularly favour licensing arrangements?

What are the long-term disadvantages to an exporter of entering into licensing agreements?

What limitations are there on an exporter attempting to license products and services overseas?

What are the different types of licence?

What are the monetary rewards of licensing?

How does an exporter find potential licensees?

What elements form the basis of a licensing agreement?

> *Chapter 9, synopsis*
> - A pathway to profits
> - When licensing is best
> - The problems of licensing
> - Practical difficulties
> - Different types of licence
> - How much can be earned?
> - Searching for licensees
> - The nature of the agreement

A PATHWAY TO PROFITS

Question **What is a licensing agreement?**

Licensing arrangements allow a company to obtain local production in an overseas market without capital investment.
In a licensing agreement, company A provides the opportunity for company B, overseas, to manufacture, market and
sell the product of company A, in return for payment.
Usually, licensing involves the transfer of technology. Without something 'special' there would be no reason for a licensee
to make payment to a licensor other than in a straight
purchase of goods or service. The payment usually takes
the form of a once-only fee, plus royalties on sales – subject
to the negotiation concluded between the two parties.
Services may also be licensed.

The licensor gives the licensee

- patent rights covering a product or process
- know-how on products or processes not covered by
  any patents
- technical advice and training
- copyrights allowing the use of a trade-mark or trade
  name.

In return, the licensee undertakes to

- produce the licensor's products covered by the licence

- to market the products in an assigned territory
- to pay a royalty and/or fee related to the volume of the product produced.

WHEN LICENSING IS BEST

Question **What marketing conditions particularly favour licensing arrangements?**

There are certain market conditions that particularly favour licensing. They are:

- Physical distribution costs make the landed price of the product with duties paid, uncompetitive.
- Import quotas and customs duties limit the development of the local market.
- Political or financial risks are disincentives to the setting up of an overseas subsidiary manufacturing company.
- Capital resources of the licensor are inadequate to set up manufacturing and marketing facilities in the local market.
- The perishable nature of the product with a limited shelf life imposes excessive constraints on distribution in the local market.
- Opportunity for cross-licensing. A return exchange of know-how and patents creates attractive business opportunities.
- Entry into a highly competitive market through a company with well-established distribution channels. Local manufacture may also be an advantage in securing government contracts.
- Opportunities through licensing exist for worldwide exploitation of new products, on a scale not possible with limited financial resources.
- Many governments favour licensing as against direct investment and manufacture, because the licensing brings technology to the country with fewer strings and conditions attached.

THE PROBLEMS OF LICENSING

Question   What are the long-term disadvantages to an exporter
of entering into licensing agreements?

The disadvantages of licensing that balance against the advantages are few, but they are important. They are:

- The licensor may establish and train a direct competitor. Licence agreements are usually for an initial period of five, seven or ten years. The agreement that is negotiated will try to preclude the subsequent setting up of a competitor factory. But loopholes are sometimes found.
- The return to the exporter – of the order of between 3 per cent and 7 per cent – is small compared to the returns that are possible with efficiently managed investment in manufacturing capacity.
- Difficulties of controlling the licensee in terms of:
  - quality control
  - extent of territory
  - marketing effort.
- Restrictions imposed by government on the remittance of royalties to the licensor.

PRACTICAL DIFFICULTIES

Question   What limitations are there on an exporter attempting
to license products and services overseas?

Provided that a would-be licensor is able to find a licensee, there are no limits to the products and services that can be licensed. Reality, however, imposes constraints. If the licensor has not fully protected his product or service by patent or copyright, a buyer will not be found.

Licences are sold in the market-place in the same way that industrial products are sold. While the body of different licence agreements have a common structure, the details of each agreement is negotiated keenly to the smallest detail. An exporter's product must usually have an impressive track record of success in the home market. Alternatively, there is an innovative service or process with convincing potential that is protected so tightly that the would-be licensor cannot gain access except through a licensing agreement.

Patents and copyrights and trade name registrations must be registered by potential licensors, not only in the home market but in every other market where business development is sought.

From the licensee's point of view, a licence fee coupled with ongoing royalty payments is worthwhile, when

- an opportunity arises to acquire a well-known brand name, with the attendant clout in the market-place
- a technological edge is possible over local competitive manufacturers
- there are opportunities for product development that are not achievable through internal development.

DIFFERENT TYPES OF LICENCE

Question   **What are the different types of licence?**

There are three basic types of licence, discussed below.

Exclusive licence   In an exclusive licence, the licensee is, for all practical purposes, in the same position as the licensor before the licence was granted. The licence is exclusive to the licensee. No one other than the licensee may carry out the operation being licensed.

Exclusivity is a frequent requirement of a licensee. Not only will he then be sure that there is no competition from other licensed producers in his country, he will also avoid competition from export sales from the licensor. In practice, safeguards are built into an exclusive licence arrangement. To ensure that the licensee devotes full attention to the arrangement, minimum royalty payment levels are set. Failure to achieve the set levels gives the licensor the right to withdraw the licence or to reduce it to the status of non-exclusive licence.

Sole licence   This is one in which a licensor grants a licence to one licensee only, but retains the right to operate the invention himself. Thus with an overseas licence the licensor retains the right to exploit the licensee's territory. As with the exclusive licence, the agreement contains provision for minimum royalty payments to ensure that the licensee operates the process to maximum mutual benefit.

Non-exclusive licence   In this case the licensor appoints a licensee but retains the right to appoint other licensees as and when he wishes. Usually the first licensee requires an assurance that the licensor does not grant a licence to other parties on more favourable terms.

Mention should be made of another type of licence, which is perhaps the most common of all, although it is seldom regarded as a licence. In the USA it is known as a *label licence*. The situation arises when there is patent protection for the 'use' of a compound for an item which is itself not patentable. The manufacturer of that item then sells it on the open market, and in so doing grants a licence to the purchasers to use it for the purpose covered by the supplier's patents. However, should someone purchase from some other source the item which itself is not patentable, and then use it for the patented use, he is obliged to take a licence and pay a royalty to the patentee.

HOW MUCH CAN BE EARNED?

Question   What are the monetary rewards of licensing?

With very few exceptions companies license technology whose development has been paid for without any expectation of licensing revenues. Thus these revenues can be treated as profit on a marginal costing basis.

The revenues can be balanced against the cost of estabishing a pure licence position, or a minority joint-venture position. The costs are clearly less than that of building fully owned additional production capacity. Also to be considered is the fact that the income earned by licensing is less than that which would be earned if direct export were possible.

There is no standard royalty rate earned by companies.

Each licence is considered on its merits. There are two main types of fees:

- single initial payment
- royalties

and a combination of the two.

Single initial payment

Typically the size of payment is calculated from the royalty expected from ten year's operation, discounted back to today's value.

The advantages to the licensor include:

- obtaining the money early
- fee not altered by underproduction
- no collection problems
- credit is possible.

The disadvantages are:

- The fee is paid at the very time that the licensee can ill afford to settle payment.
- Difficulties are likely to arise in obtaining increased monies if the plant subsequently shows the potential for increased capacity.

Royalty

Royalty is the most frequently adopted payment, particularly for the manufacturer of components using a licensed process in an existing factory. An advantage is a low early commitment. Another advantage is that revenue varies with output. There is no fixed royalty rate. It varies from between 3 per cent and 7 per cent.

Before negotiations on the actual terms of a licence agreement begin, it is necessary for a licensee to evaluate the technology being offered. At this stage a secrecy agreement is often necessary. The potential licensee enters into a binding commitment not to make use of the information supplied except at such time as a licence agreement is subsequently concluded between the two parties.

THE SEARCH FOR LICENSEES

Question   **How does an exporter find potential licensees?**

The search for a licensee overseas is in many ways comparable to the search for a good agent or distributor. But there are a number of limiting factors. For example, the licensee must have the financial and manufacturing or marketing clout to be able to fulful a licensing agreement. A good agent does not need such financial strength.

The starting point is the industry itself. Who in the market-place overseas is well placed to market the product or service to be licensed. A short list of obvious choices is prepared. A profile of each company is researched and build up.

A licence may be for a process at the raw-material stage of production, for a stage in assembly, or for a finished product. The initial search for a licensee begins in the over-seas market-place. The company is likely to have a comparable position in the market-place to the licensor or the licensor's distributors in the home market. But potential licensees can be companies wishing to move from adjacent market segments into fresh fields. Methodically, the search for licen-sees is spread laterally and vertically within the industry.

When a short list of potential licensees is compiled, enquiries are carried out to rate the companies or individuals in terms of their drive, capabilities and resources. An ap-proach is then made directly.

Sometimes a point in negotiations is reached when the licensor is reluctant to disclose further information about his company without some commitment from the potential licensee. It is usual at that stage for the other party to enter an agreement not to take benefit from the discussions other than through the prescribed channels.

THE NATURE OF THE AGREEMENT

Question **What elements form the basis of a licensing agreement?**

As with all binding agreements, the final document should be prepared by a person with appropriate legal and

commercial experience and qualifications. But the body of
the document reflects the needs and commitments of both
parties. The legal format structures the manner in which
the relationship to be established becomes binding.

The following aspects are usually incorporated in a licence
agreement:

- The subject of the agreement. The product, service
  or process that is being licensed is defined clearly and
  precisely.
- The territory describes the area in which the licensee
  is permitted to work. The precise circumstances in
  which the licensee is able to trade, directly or indirectly
  outside of the prescribed boundaries, are given.
- The term of the agreement – for five, seven, ten or
  fifteen years – is stated.
- Exclusivity basis is defined as arranged between the
  parties.
- The language in which the agreement is to be formulated and interpreted is specified, including the
  arrangements appropriate to contingent translation
  requirements.
- The obligations of the licensor are set out. They relate
  to the technology and the supply of know-how.
- The obligations of the licensee. The details are comprehensive covering:
    - quality standards required
    - opportunities for licensor to monitor and inspect
      licensee activities and records
    - payment terms, currency and methods of
      payment
    - protection of licensor's patents and copyrights
    - indemnification of licensor against claim
    - respect of the terms and conditions of the licence
      agreement
    - confidentiality
    - circumstances under which the licence is revoked
      or withdrawn
    - performance of the licensee on termination of
      the agreement, in respect of the property,
      trademarks and technology of the licensor

- assignment of the agreement
- product and process development
- compliance with local legal, safety and health requirements
- performance targets, with the minimum levels that must be achieved.
- acceptance of arbitration to determine disputes that are not resolved.

Licensing, for the exporter equipped with an appropriate product service or process, and protected by relevant patent, is a worthwhile activity. The initial efforts are rewarded by ongoing royalty payments and consolidation of export markets.

An example of a licence agreement between Laser Beam Technology Ltd and Hochberg GmBH is reproduced with permission as an appendix to this chapter.

APPENDIX TO CHAPTER 9: SPECIMEN LICENCE AGREEMENT

Date: 1st January 1986
Between: Laser Beam Technology Ltd of Carlton Vale, Slough, Berks (hereinafter defined as 'ABCD') and Hochberg GmBH (hereinafter defined as 'the Licensee')

1. Definitions

In this Agreement:

'Products' means the items specified in the First Schedule hereto as supplied by ABCD hereunder in the English language form and as translated hereunder by the Licensee into the French or German language.

'Territory' means Switzerland.

'Term' means the period commencing on the date hereof and ending either on 31st December 1996 or on the earlier determination of this Agreement in accordance with the provisions hereinafter contained.

2. Licence

Subject to the performance by the Licensee of its agreements herein ABCD hereby grants to the Licensee during the Term:

(a) the exclusive right to sell in the Territory copies of the Product numbered 1 in the First Schedule hereto on the following terms and conditions and

(b) the non-exclusive right to sell in the Territory copies of the Products numbered 2 and 3 in the First Schedule hereto on the following terms and conditions and

(c) the right, but only for the purpose of exercising the rights contained in sub-clauses (a) and (b) above, to copy, reproduce or translate into the French and German languages the English language version of the Products supplied by ABCD hereunder.

3. Agreements by ABCD

ABCD agrees:

(a) to supply on loan to the Licensee a master copy in the English language of each of the Products and to supply a copy of any corrected or improved version of any of the Products which becomes available during the Term, and

(b) Subject to the performance by the Licensee of its agreements herein and with a view to ensuring that the Product described in the First Schedule hereto as LB183 functions as specified in the relevant Instruction Manual, therefore to endeavour at its own expense and within a reasonable time to correct any malfunction in any copy thereof (other than errors resulting from the said translations) of which written notice is given by the Licensee to ABCD within one year of the delivery of such copy by the Licensee to its customer *PROVIDED THAT* save as aforesaid ABCD will not be responsible for the installation or servicing of any of the Products or any copy thereof.

4. Agreements by the Licensee

The Licensee agrees with ABCD at all times during the continuance in force of this Agreement to observe and perform the terms and conditions hereof and in particular

(a)   at its own expense to use its best endeavours to promote and extend the sale of copies of the Products throughout the Territory and to give pre-sale and post-sale promotion and support therefor and to provide such suitable installation and training facilities as ABCD may reasonably require;

(b)   not to sell any copy of the Products to any person at a price less than that specified opposite the description of each Product in the First Schedule hereto;

(c)   to include in all contracts or arrangements made by it for the sale of any copy of any Product to any person the provision referred to in the Second Schedule hereto *AND* without limiting the generality of the foregoing (to the extent that under the provisions of the law applicable to the Licensee's contracts with its customers they are not inconsistent with the foregoing requirements) the Terms and Conditions annexed hereto;

(d)   fully and effectually to indemnify ABCD and to keep it indemnified against all claims or demands and against all expenses incurred in relation thereto by reason of any loss or damage suffered by any person (whether or not by reason of the negligence of the Licensee or any servant or agent of it) arising out of the use, non-use or malfunction of or any error or fault in the said French or German language translations of the Products and any copies thereof;

(e)   to pay to ABCD at a United Kingdom bank (or such other place as may be nominated by ABCD) in sterling converted at the rate of exchange prevailing at the time payment is made sums equal to 5% of the sale price of each copy of the Products charged by the Licensee to its customers, such payment to be made either not later than 30 days after payment to the Licensee of such sale price or 3 months after supply by the Licensee of each copy of each of the Products (as the case may be), whichever is earlier and pending payment to ABCD to hold all monies due to it in a separate trust account;

(f) to keep full proper and up-to-date books of account and records showing clearly all transactions, proceedings and enquiries relating to the sale of copies of the Products and the charges therefor and to allow ABCD and those authorized by it to inspect such accounts and take copies thereof:

(g) to keep full details (including copies of all contracts) concerning the sales of the copies of the Products and the number and location of copies of the Products and produce such details to ABCD on request;

(h) not to use, copy, reproduce or otherwise exploit or deal with the Products otherwise than by the outright sale of copies of the Products to its customers within the Territory during the Term on the terms hereof and for demonstration and testing purposes in connection with sales of copies of the Products *AND* (without limiting the generality of the foregoing) not itself to use nor permit any other person to use the Products or any copy thereof unless it or such other person (as the case may be) has purchased a copy of the Products on the terms of this Agreement and such use is in accordance with the terms of this Agreement;

(i) not to sell or deal with either of the instruction manuals separately from LB183 to which they relate;

(j) not to sell copies of the Products outside the Territory nor allow them to be sold outside or sold for use outside the Territory *SAVE THAT* copies of the Products may be sold to an international company having its head office in the Territory for such Company's own personal use in its offices outside the Territory;

(k) to take such action as it or ABCD shall consider necessary to enforce ABCD's or the Licensee's rights under the Licensee's sale agreements with its customers;

(l) to notify ABCD immediately of any infringement of ABCD's copyrights rights in the nature of copyright or of any other rights referred to in sub-clauses 7 (a) and (b) below and of any improper or wrongful use of or infringement of ABCD's patents, trade marks, emblems, designs or other similar commercial monopoly rights which the Licensee knows or suspects has taken place or may take place and to use every reasonable effort to safeguard the property rights of ABCD and at ABCD's request to assist ABCD in taking all steps desirable to protect and enforce ABCD's rights in the Territory;

(m)   at its expense to return to ABCD the Products and all copies of the Products in the Licensee's possession or under its control at the termination of this Agreement howsoever caused and all copies of the Products coming into its possession or control at any time thereafter;

(n)   to procure that the Products and all copies of the Products sold or dealt with by the Licensee contain the following copyright notice in a prominent position so as to give notice of copyright protection '© Laser Beam Technology Ltd 1984' or such other notice as ABCD may require and *FURTHER AGREES* at the Licensee's expense to take such action *AND* to include in the Products and all copies of the Products and in its sale agreements with it customers such other provisions as may be appropriate to protect ABCD's copyright rights in the nature of copyright and other property rights in the Products;

(o)   that all sales of copies of the Products by it will be at arms length on the best commercial terms;

(p)   in all matters to act loyally and faithfully to ABCD and in any matter in which its obligations are not specifically defined by this Agreement to act in such manner as it reasonably considers to be most beneficial to the interests of ABCD.

5. Exclusion of Liability

(a)   ABCD shall not be responsible for any loss or damage caused to the Licensee or save as set out in sub-clause (b) below to any other person nor for any loss of profit or consequential loss or damage howsoever arising (whether or not by reason of the negligence of ABCD or any servant or agent of it or otherwise) by reason of any use or malfunction of, or the inability to use, or any error or fault in, any of the Products or any copy thereof and all express or implied warranties or conditions statutory or otherwise as to the quality or fitness of any of the Products or any copies thereof for any purpose or their compliance with any description or specification are hereby expressly excluded.

(b) Notwithstanding the provisions of sub-clause (a) above but subject to the provisions of sub-clause (c) below ABCD agrees to indemnify the Licensee (subject to the terms of the PROVISO hereinafter set out) against one half of either

(i) any sum of damages awarded against the Licensee by a Court of Law (applying the Law of Switzerland) to a Purchaser of a copy of any of the Products from the Licensee pursuant to the provisions of this Licence Agreement representing loss or damage suffered by that Purchaser as a direct consequence of any error or fault in or malfunction of the said English language version of the Product concerned as a result of which the Product does not function as specified in the relevant instruction manual therefor; or

(ii) any compensation paid by the Licensee on the advice of a Swiss lawyer qualified at least ten years and experienced in the particular field to which the claim relates to compromise or settle any claim which if successful would result in the award of damages to a Purchaser of any copy of any of the Products from the Licensee pursuant to the provisions of this Licence Agreement representing loss or damage as aforesaid. *PROVIDED THAT* such lawyer shall have advised the Licensee that such claim is more likely to succeed than to fail and *PROVIDED ALSO* that ABCD shall have given its prior written consent to the payment of such compensation (such consent not to be unreasonably withheld)

PROVIDED THAT in no event shall ABCD's liability under this sub-clause in respect of any such damages or compensation exceed the sterling sum received by ABCD from the Licensee in respect of the sale of the copy of the Product concerned to that Purchaser.

(c) The indemnity given by ABCD pursuant to the provisions of sub-clause (b) above is conditional both on the Licensee performing all its agreements and obligations contained in this Licence Agreement and on the Purchaser concerned performing and observing all its agreements and obligations contained in its agreement with the Licensee relating to the sale to the Purchaser of the copy of the Product concerned.

(d)　(i) The payment of any sum by ABCD pursuant to the indemnity hereinbefore contained shall be converted at the rate of exchange prevailing at the time payment is made; and

(ii) for the purpose of calculating whether ABCD's liability pursuant to the indemnity contained in sub-clause (b) above would exceed the said sterling sum received by ABCD from the Licensee as therein referred to, the relevant rate of exchange shall be that prevailing on the day when ABCD makes payment to the Licensee pursuant to its said indemnity.

(e)　The Licensee will forthwith notify ABCD of any claim which it knows is being made against it or suspects may be made against it and which may result in ABCD becoming liable to make payment under the indemnity hereinbefore contained and without prejudice to the provisions of sub-clause (b) (ii) above the Licensee will keep ABCD fully informed as to all matters and will supply ABCD with copies of all documents relating to any such claim and will consult with ABCD and pay due regard to its views concerning the defence to any such claim or any other action to be taken in regard to any such claim.

6. ABCD's Rights in the Territory

ABCD and any one authorized by it shall be entitled to grant to any company having its head office outside the Territory the right for that Company and any associated company (as that expression is defined in Section 302 of the Income and Corporation Taxes Act 1970) to use copies of the Products or any of them in its or their place of business within the Territory.

7. Copyright

(a)　the Licensee hereby as beneficial owner

(i) agrees to assign to ABCD the property in the said French and German language translations of the Products; and

(ii) hereby assigns to ABCD by way of present and future assignment of copyright the entire copyright and all rights in the nature of copyright subsisting now or at any time in the future throughout the world in the said French and German language translations of the Products to hold the same unto ABCD absolutely throughout the world for the full term of copyright and all extensions and renewals thereof.

(b) ABCD will retail all other copyright rights in the nature of copyright and all other property rights in the Products and all copies thereof.

(c) the Licensee agrees to sign or execute such further documents or deeds as ABCD shall require to confirm the assignments contained in sub-clause (a) hereof.

8. Confidentiality

The Licensee acknowledges the confidential nature of the know-how and information contained in the Products and agrees that the supply thereof pursuant to this Agreement will constitute a disclosure thereof to the Licensee in confidence and agrees not at any time during or after the termination of this Agreement to divulge any such know-how or information to any other person except as is necessary by virtue of the exercise of its rights under this Agreement.

9. Trials

The Licensee shall be entitled to supply one copy of each of the Products to a prospective customer on a trial basis without incurring any liability to make payment to ABCD pursuant to sub-clause 4(e) above *PROVIDED THAT* the period for which the customer has such copy on trial shall not exceed two months and *PROVIDED FURTHER THAT* as a condition precedent the Licensee shall prior to supplying any such copy enter into an agreement with such prospective customer containing the provisions referred to in the Second Schedule hereto and to the extent aforesaid the said Terms and Conditions annexed hereto.

10. Termination

Notwithstanding any other provision of this Agreement this Agreement may be terminated:
(a)   at any time by the mutual consent of the parites;
(b)   by ABCD forthwith by giving written notice to the Licensee
      (i) if the Licensee shall fail in any calendar year of the Term to sell one copy of each of the Products marked * in the First Schedule or
      (ii) if the Licensee is in breach of any term or condition of this Agreement, or (iii) if the Licensee enters into liquidation (whether compulsory or voluntarily) or makes any arrangement or composition with its creditors or has a Receiver appointed over all or any of its assets or takes or suffers any similar action in consequence of debt in any jurisdiction.

11. The termination of this Agreement whensoever occurring or for whatever cause shall be without prejudice to the rights of the parties accrued due.

12. Agency

Nothing in this Agreement shall constitute or be deemed to constitute a partnership between the parties nor be construed as constituting the Licensee an agent of ABCD and the Licensee will not represent itself as an agent of ABCD.

13. Assignment

This Agreement is personal to the Licensee and may not be assigned or otherwise dealt with by it nor may the Licensee assign or purport to assign or otherwise deal with the benefit of its sale agreements with it customers.

14. Waiver

The waiver by ABCD of any breach by the Licensee of any of its agreements warranties or undertakings herein shall not prevent the subsequent enforcement of its rights in

respect of such breach and shall not be deemed to be a waiver
of any subsequent breach.

15. Law

This Agreement shall constitute the entire agreement
between the parties and shall be governed by and construed
in accordance with the provisions of English Law. The
headings of the clauses do not form part of the Agreement
between the parties.

16. Notices

All notices by either party hereunder shall be in writing
addressed to the other party at its above address (or such
other address as may from time to time be notified to the
other party) and if sent by first-class pre-paid post shall be
deemed to have been delivered 72 hours after posting.

17. VAT

ABCD shall be entitled to charge VAT at the rate from
time to time in force on all payments to be made by the
Licensee hereunder.

THE FIRST SCHEDULE above referred to

 1*. LB183 20,000 Swiss Francs per copy
 2. Manual M183 No charge
 3. Manual M184 50 Swiss Francs per copy

*THE SECOND SCHEDULE above referred to WITHOUT
PREJUDICE* to the provisions of the Agreement to which
this Schedule is attached the Licensee will include in each
of its agreements for sale of and use on trial of copies of
the Products or any of them suitable provisions:

(a) prohibiting the user from using or authorizing or permitting the use of any copy of the Products for any
purpose other than the user's own commercial use at
the user's own premises;

(b) prohibiting the user from making or authorizing or
permitting the making of any copy or reproduction of
the Products or any part thereof;

(c)   prohibiting the user from at any time communicating or authorizing or permitting the communication of any know-how or information contained in the Products to any other person;

(d)   for the protection of ABCD's copyright and other rights in the nature of copyright in the Products and all copies thereof.

AS WITNESS the hands of the duly authorized representatives of the parties

SIGNED by
on behalf of ABCD in
the presence of:-
SIGNED by
on behalf of the
LICENSEE in the presence of:

TERMS AND CONDITIONS

1.   The property in the Packages shall pass from [the Licensee] to the Buyer only upon due payment of the Total Amount Due hereunder.

2.   With a view to ensuring that the Package(s) function(s) as specified in the associated manuals [the Licensee] shall at its own expense and within a reasonable time correct any malfunction of which notice is given in writing by the Buyer to [the Licensee] within one year after the date of delivery of the Package(s).

3.   All copyright and other rights in the nature of copyright in the Package(s) and the associated manuals are and shall remain vested in Laser Beam Technology Ltd ('ABCD') and the Buyer is only authorized to copy or reproduce the Package(s) and the associated manuals or any part thereof as and when necessary for its own use at the computer installation address(es) named on the face of this form and for no other person whatsoever.

4.   The Buyer acknowledges the confidential nature of the know-how and information contained in the Package(s) and the associated manuals, and delivery of the Package(s) by [the Licensee] will constitute a disclosure

thereof to the Buyer in confidence. The Buyer accordingly undertakes with [the Licensee] that it will not communicate any of such know-how and information to any other person firm or company.

5. The Buyer shall not resell or in any way dispose or part with possession of or authorize the use copying or reproduction of the Package(s) or the associated manuals or any part thereof to or by any other person firm or company.

SUMMARY

Question   What is a licensing agreement?

Answer   A licensing agreement is an arrangement whereby company A provides the opportunity for company B to manufacture, and/or market and sell locally the product or service of company A. Licensing usually involves the transfer of technology.

Question What marketing conditions particularly favour licensing arrangements?

Answer   The conditions favouring licensing agreements arise when there are factors weighing against direct export, such as high physical distribution costs, political and financial constraints.

Question   What are the long-term disadvantages to an exporter of entering into licensing agreements?

Answer   The principal disadvantages of licensing are (1) the licensor may be training a future competitor, (2) profitability is less than through efficient direct marketing and (3) there may be difficulties in controlling the quality of the licensed product or service.

Question   What constraints exist for an exporter attempting to license products and services overseas?

Answer   If a licensor has not fully protected his product or service by patent or copyright, difficulties are likely in finding a licensee. It is also important that the product or service benefits the licensee in ways which cannot be achieved by other means.

Question   What are the different types of licence?

Answer   There are three basic types of licence: an exclusive licence, a sole licence and a non-exclusive licence.

Question   What are the monetary rewards of licensing?

Answer   The rewards of licensing are a single initial payment, royalties or a combination of the two.

Question   How does an exporter find potential licensees?

Answer   The search for a licensee is comparable to the search for an agent or a distributor.

Question   What elements form the basis of a licensing agreement?

Answer   A licensing agreement clearly defines (1) the product, service or process that is licensed, (2) the financial and legal terms of the licence, and (3) the obligations of the licensor and the licensee.

10 'Big business' export activities

Before reading the chapter, answer the following test questions. The answers are worked through in the text. Question and answer are provided together at the end of the chapter as a summary.

QUESTIONS

How is manufacturing capacity in an overseas market established?

What advantages are enjoyed by exporting firms with manufacturing capacity overseas?

What are the disadvantages to an exporter of establishing manufacturing capacity overseas?

What marketing opportunities enables the established exporter to progress to large-scale business overseas?

What does exporting through 'own-label manufacture' mean?

What is a management contract?

What is an effective alternative to creating a wholly owned manufacturing operation overseas?

When investment and expenditure are not critical factors, what opportunities are there for generating overseas sources of revenue?

Chapter 10 synopsis

- When to manufacture on the spot
- How to take advantage
- Disadvantages
- Opportunities for large-scale business
- Marginal export business
- Exporting management services
- Working with others
- Buying overseas assets

WHEN TO MANUFACTURE ON THE SPOT

Question **How is manufacturing capacity in an overseas market established?**

The starting point of export business is often scant market research and an appointed agent. With application and effort business grows. Other agents are appointed, or distributors are appointed.

Figure 10.1 illustrates the process. When the products are consumer goods, the next step is the opening of a break bulk depot in the local market so that goods may be shipped in bulk to reduce distribution costs. If exports are industrial products, there is similarly a requirement for storage of parts stock and facilities for the supply of service back-up.

The volume of export business grows. To control that business effectively a point is reached where a permanent presence in the market-place is needed. A marketing/sales office fulfils this function. When it is appropriate the office or offices service as a break bulk depot too. An expatriate employee of the export company is domiciled in the territory. A sales force of local nationals is built up, because the most effective sales are achieved when the products are sold by people speaking the same language as the customer and drawn from the same culture.

A marketing office is well placed, too, to gather research data from the field. Export success is not usually achieved without the capacity to predict and adapt to market trends and needs. From time to time there are many aspects of change in the market-place – changes in legislation, in health and safety requirements, in customs tariffs, in quotas and in taxation requirements.

At the stage of progress where the need for a marketing office becomes apparent, there are already established connections in the market-place. There is likely to be an agent or a network of agents. There may be one or more distributors. Additionally there is the customer base. Logically the marketing office is set up in conjunction with a person or company with whom a mutually rewarding business relationship already exists.

As business increases to an even greater volume the next stage of development is a plant for either

(a) the assembly of the product exported in knocked down form
(b) manufacture of the product
(c) or a combination of (a) and (b).

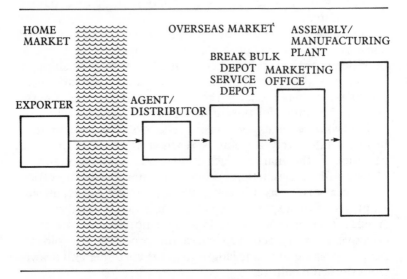

Figure 10.1 A pathway to manufacturing capacity overseas (note: The marketing office may be established before a break bulk depot)

HOW TO TAKE ADVANTAGE

Question **What advantages are enjoyed by exporting firms with manufacturing capacity overseas?**

The decision to manufacture overseas is a big one. There are advantages to manufacture over direct exports, but there must be investment. Financial resources are needed. So are management resources and R&D capacity to make sure that the product exactly matches the overseas customer's needs. By commencing manufacturing operations in markets other than the home market, companies fall into the category of multinational companies. There are advantages, unique to multinational companies, some of which are described below.

The following factors are persuasive in establishing an overseas factory:

- Reduced physical distribution costs. Freight, packaging and handling costs can be substantially reduced. Another important advantage is that delivery times are reduced. Exporters gain reputations for poor delivery and poor service very quickly, even with one bad experience. That reputation is difficult to live down. Delivery from within the market-place contributes to reliability. The factory may be well placed for deliveries to adjacent export markets.

- Cost savings from local cheap labour. In some overseas markets there is a considerable wage differential. Taking advantage of lower labour costs is a pathway to competitive pricing.

- Cost savings from cheaper local components or raw materials. As with low labour costs, this helps achieve lower selling prices.

- Removal of the requirement to pay import duties. Manufacture provides price competitiveness against other exporters who are obliged to pay the customs duties when their goods are imported.

- Lobbying of the local market's national government to impose import duties, if none exist. Once an exporter is established in a market through a manufacturing base, it is desirable to protect the industry from other exporters.

- Opportunities for ongoing market research data collection. Data collection, analysis and storage can be planned as an integral part of the manufacturing base.
- The practice of transfer pricing. Multinational companies set prices for the 'sale' or transfer of goods, or component parts, between subsidiary or associate companies of the world. In this way maximum profits for the whole group are declared in the country where liability for taxation is least.

DISADVANTAGES

Question   What are the disadvantages to an exporter of establishing manufacturing capacity overseas?

Companies making the decision to join the league of 'multinational' organizations expose themselves to certain risks. The risks are:

- Sequestration of assets overseas following political changes in the host country. The directors of the company are divested of their control over the overseas factory. This happens suddenly and dramatically, when there is civil unrest; or over a set period of time when a new government seeks rigid national independence.
- Exchange control regulations prevent repatriation of royalties and profits. When a country moves into an adverse balance of trade, imposition of stringent exchange control regulations is one of a number of measures open to government to redress the balance.
- Reduced overall performance. A requirement for profitable international trade is a solid, well-managed home base. If management and financial resources are diluted, overall performance can suffer. Successful manufacture overseas requires specialist skills – especially if the new factory is in a market with a different culture and a different language.

OPPORTUNITIES FOR LARGE-SCALE BUSINESS

Question   What marketing opportunities enable the established exporter to progress to large-scale business overseas?

Large-scale opportunities to develop business overseas are possible through consortia. The fields of activity are usually in engineering, construction or petrochemicals, but there are also successes in other fields such as foods, armaments and transportation.

In a consortium, manufacturers of complementary products join together with suppliers of complementary services. The services are finance, or specialist management skills, or insurance and credit insurance. There are a number of advantages to a consortium that are not enjoyed by individual member companies acting alone:

- A synergy deriving from the nature and breadth of the consortium input.
- A sharing of risk. Individual commitment is restricted with attractive prospects of substantial returns.
- A sharing of technical resources. Consortium objectives may not be achievable by one member company alone without severely stretching the company's resources.
- Opportunities of support at senior government level. A recent important power plant deal was signed between the government of the Chinese People's Republic and a United Kingdom consortium. The consortium was headed by a senior official of the Department of Trade and Industry.
- International marketing know-how. Membership of a consortium provides a short-cut to acquiring specialist marketing skills.
- Opportunities for long-term planning. The projected large-scale business usually associated with consortia provides opportunities for detailed planning.
- Reduction in export sales overheads. Consortia activities lead to sharing of some of the fixed costs attendant upon maintaining a presence overseas.
- Penetration of new export markets. The experience and support of fellow consortia members opens up

target-market horizons that would not be considered by member companies acting alone.

Consortia can have different objectives. These may be as follows:

A large scale capital project   Examples are roadway transportation infrastructure, an airport, a hospital, a deep-water port.

A turnkey project   In a turnkey project the car production factory, or the radio broadcasting station, or the oil refinery – whatever is the project objective – is built from scratch. Operatives and management are hired, trained and integrated into the project organization. Lines of component and material supply, and the distribution channels for the manufactured products, are developed. When the project is manned and working to agreed levels it is handed over to the client. Various methods of payment for turnkey projects exist, as a function of the needs and resources of the parties. It can be by an initial up-front payment on signing of contract, followed by stage payments as construction proceeds. Royalties on the factory production may then form part of the deal, especially where technology is licensed to the turnkey project purchasers. A variation, where the host has difficulties in providing hard currency, is royalty payments in the form of a regular supply of the goods produced by the factory or plant that has been built.

ADDITIONAL EXPORT BUSINESS

Question   What does exporting through 'own-label manufacture' mean?

Outside of the traditional export channels are all the other activities devised by businessmen to increase their business. 'Own-label manufacture' is one such activity. A manufacturer sells his product in bulk to another, packaged in the livery of the purchaser. The original manufacturer has no part in the marketing of the product. His responsibility is solely to provide production capacity. In the home market, own-label sales are increasingly made to supermarket chains. The customer strikes a tough bargain with the supplier. The benefits of a keen price are then passed on to the captive market of consumers shopping in the supermarket.

A manufacturer in the home market has surplus capacity. He researches export markets to identify where a similar product or products to his own are sold. He then identifies the local manufacturers in that market and makes contact. Alternatively, the manufacturer advertises, through the trade association of the local market, that production capacity is available.

Own-label sales are an attractive supplement to the manufacturer's own business turnover. But there are certain factors that must be considered carefully:

- The agreed price level is likely to be extremely keen.
- The manufacturer has no control in the market-place. Future business is entirely dependent on the customer placing repeat business.
- The more own-label business the manufacturer transacts, the stronger the customer becomes in the market-place. This in itself does not matter, until such time as the manufacturer decides to export to the local market directly. He then faces a competitor strongly entrenched in the market-place, with a product that is identical to his own.

In most markets the product specification, quality, size, shape and packaging reflect the needs of the local customer. To undertake own-label supply the production line must be able to accommodate such requirements. One own-label product exported in bulk from the UK to Germany is dog food. The product specification is identical to that marketed in the UK.

EXPORTING MANAGEMENT SKILLS

Question **What is a management contract?**

Management skills are a product in the same way that a table or a pair of trousers are products. It is possible to export management skills in the same way that products are exported. A management contract is an agreement whereby a company manages some or all of the operations of another company. The returns are a fee and usually a share of the profits.

Hilton hotels are an example of management contracts. Overseas, the hotels are built by local investment. The hotels are then managed by the Hilton Hotels Corporation with complete responsibility for achieving profitability. Staff are recruited, trained and managed by the Hilton group. Visitors to the hotel stay at a 'Hilton' hotel, and the financial basis of the arrangements does not intrude.

Management contracts are common in oil exploration and also in airline-servicing operations.

The advantages of management contracts are that they provide a means of market entry overseas without capital investment. As risk-free exporting, management contracts are therefore an attractive option. Such disadvantages as exist are a function of the business itself. Management involves the recruitment, employment and motivation of skilled personnel. Provided that these activities are under control, disadvantages can be contained.

WORKING WITH OTHERS

Question **What is an effective alternative to creating a wholly owned manufacturing operation overseas?**

An alternative course of action to manufacturing overseas through a wholly owned subsidiary is a *joint venture*. In some markets, for example the Middle East, joint venture is not an option but a mandatory requirement. An international joint venture is an association by a company with another company or companies overseas. The companies share the tasks of manufacture, marketing, distribution and financing. The proportion of the responsibilities can vary widely. It is a matter of agreement between the parties and the statutory regulations of the host country.

Usually a feature of a joint venture is that no single party has a controlling share so that management control is shared. There are certain circumstances where a joint venture operation is the most appropriate method of entering an export market. For example, where

- the exporter has no local marketing expertise.
- a joint venture is able to provide established distribution channels
- management skills are limited (language capabilities are included under this heading)
- consumer attitudes favour products manufactured locally to those imported
- there are opportunities of relief from import duties and tariffs
- a joint venture relationship is expedient to safeguard lines of supply of raw materials owned by one of the parties.

A disadvantage of joint venture activities is that conflict, or imagined conflict, of interest may arise. There are likely to be national differences of culture and behaviour ethics. Possibly there are even differences in styles of transacting business. Communication is another factor. Because of limited language capability, it is not possible to maintain communication at a desired level.

It is difficult to withdraw from a joint venture operation once commenced, without sustaining penalties and loss. The exporter is cautioned to do the necessary homework thoroughly. Not least, the exporter should speak to companies with experience of joint venture operations.

BUYING OVERSEAS ASSETS

Question **When investment and expenditure are not critical factors, what opportunities are there for generating overseas sources of revenue?**

Opportunities to gain ownership of sources of income overseas lie in *acquisition*. The controlling interest in the shares of an overseas manufacturer or supplier of services is purchased. When this is possible – and sometimes local legislation prohibits such transactions – there are sound advantages to the purchaser.

Immediate access to the market is gained. Ready-made distribution channels are available. Production capacity can be used to accommodate the purchaser's other product lines.

There is ready-made research data on market trends and potential. Immediate management and local marketing skills are acquired.

When the purchasers' shares are quoted on the stock exchange it may be possible to effect the purchase of the local company through a share issue. In this case the obligations of cash payment are kept to a minimum.

When circumstances are propitious for an overseas acquisition, the disadvantages are considerably less than the advantages. Two disadvantages are

- the problems of absorbing an independent management structure into the corporate framework
- the tax and investment concessions associated with investment in start-up operations overseas are not applicable.

SUMMARY

Question　How is manufacturing capacity in an overseas market established?

Answer　Appointed agents or distributors are the starting point overseas. The next stage is a presence in the overseas market with a marketing office or a depot. From this manufacturing can follow.

Question　What advantages are enjoyed by exporting firms with manufacturing capacity overseas?

Answer　True multinational status can bring extra profitability. Such profits are achieved through reduced manufacturing or distribution costs, from transfer pricing opportunities and from protection against liability for tariff duties and taxes.

Question　What are the disadvantages to an exporter of establishing manufacturing capacity overseas?

Answer　Manufacturing capacity overseas exposes an exporter to three primary areas of risk: adverse political change, adverse financial controls imposed by the host country, and diminished management effectiveness through excessive demands on human and material resources.

Question **What marketing opportunities enable the established exporter to progress to large-scale business overseas?**

Answer Opportunities for large-scale business arise through a consortium of companies and organizations providing complementary products, services and specialist skills.

Question **What does exporting through 'own-label manufacture' mean?**

Answer A home-market manufacturer is exporting through own-label manufacture when a product is sold overseas in bulk in the purchaser's livery. All marketing and distribution of the product is carried out by the purchaser.

Question **What is a management contract?**

Answer A management contract is a method of exporting specific management skills. The management company contracts to undertake an assignment overseas in return for financial reward. The assignments tend to be in the areas of manufacturing; oil or mineral exploration; and service operation and maintenance.

Question **What is an effective alternative to creating a wholly owned manufacturing operation overseas?**

Answer A joint venture with a local partner can offer a number of significant advantages particularly in respect of local marketing distribution and expertise. Commercial and political risks are shared. Disadvantages may arise from discord between the partners due to conflicts of interest.

Question When investment and expenditure are not critical factors, what opportunities are there for generating overseas sources of revenue?

Answer Acquisition offers opportunities to secure overseas sources of revenue. The controlling interest in the shares of profitable local companies are purchased. Ideally the structure of such companies will integrate beneficially with the export and production resources of the purchaser.

11 Selling to Eastern bloc countries

Before reading the chapter, answer the following test questions. The answers are worked through in the text. Question and answer are provided together at the end of the chapter as a summary.

QUESTIONS

In what way does trading with Eastern markets differ from trading with Western markets?

COMECON is associated with trade with the East. What does it mean?

In view of Eastern bloc countries being planned economies, what is the best way to carry out preliminary market research?

What is the best approach for a would-be exporter to Eastern Europe?

Does an exporter transact business with all Eastern bloc countries in the same way?

Chapter 11 synopsis

- Eastern European trade requirements
- What is COMECON?
- Researching in Eastern Europe
- Overcoming difficulties
- Degrees of difference

EASTERN EUROPEAN TRADE REQUIREMENTS

Question In what way does trading with Eastern markets differ from trading with Western markets?

The peoples of the East and the peoples of the West basically have similar appetites. As consumers they need food to eat, clothes to wear and some modes of transport. There are of course cultural differences.

A significant difference is in the method of trading. Foreign trade in Eastern bloc countries is a state monopoly. It is centrally planned. Eastern bloc countries place orders in the West only when requirements cannot be met from domestic sources. The USSR and her satellite countries suffer from a chronic shortage of hard currency. There are many demands on the hard currency that is available. Allocation of such funds is meticulously planned within five-year plans and subordinate annual plans. There are no contingency exceptions. Ad hoc purchases are unlikely to be made – no matter what the circumstances.

An example will illustrate this. A businessman in the UK manufactures specialist insulation panels. He reads in the trade press that a factory in Australia, with the same production line, is razed to the ground by fire. The business-man telexes his agent to call and offer supplies from the UK. If there is no agent, the businessman takes an aeroplane and calls on the Australian manufacturer. Business is likely to result. The initiative is rewarded. An urgent customer need is exactly satisfied. If, however, the businessman were to read that a similar factory had burned down in the Soviet Union, there is no possibility that ad hoc purchases could be made for supplies from the UK, no matter how urgently required.

In this example there are further reasons why a Western-style initiative would not succeed. First, it is unlikely that details of such a fire would ever be published overseas. Indeed, details of the hard-currency allocations of the five-year plans are not even published.

Second, agents are not as commonplace and free as in Western countries. Local agents, in the form of Russian citizens, cannot be appointed, although a type of representation is possible. In Russia there are currently only two established British trading companies acting as agents. There are also some Moscow-based foreign trading companies (e.g. Belgian or Italian). There is also the foreign-trade organization Sovincentr that provides a service in which foreign companies are represented. But the relationship is formal.

Third, it is unlikely that a businessman unknown to the appropriate state department would secure a visa to visit the scene of the fire.

WHAT IS COMECON?

Question COMECON is associated with trade with the East. What does it mean?

The term COMECON is loosely used to refer to the Council for Mutual Economic Assistance. The correct acronym is CMEA. The two acronyms are used interchangeably in everyday language, but as a courtesy to an East European national it is best to use only CMEA. Its members are East Germany, USSR, Romania, Czechoslovakia, Poland, Bulgaria, Hungary, Cuba and Vietnam. Yugoslavia attends meetings as an observer.

The objective of COMECON is the expansion of foreign trade through economic co-operation. Information is exchanged and recommendations are made through several permanent commissions. The commissions are each responsible for different industrial sectors and are concerned with economic data, technical information, research, production targets, and so on.

All trade within CMEA countries and most trade with developing countries is transacted in soft currency or under bilateral clearing arrangements.

Because of the shortage of hard currency for trading with the West, allocation is made on the basis of urgent priorities. For example, in Russia allocation is in response to requests from the different ministries which want to purchase equipment, materials or products from the West. Apart from a few basic raw materials and commodities – such as wheat, natural rubber, wool and tin – priorities go to technically

sophisticated machinery and equipment in the chemical
energy and automotive sectors. The Soviet government is
particularly concerned to increase industrial productivity
through automation and the modernization of existing plants.

Other priorities are with agriculture, food-processing and
packaging sectors. For this reason, consumer goods have
lower priorities in terms of hard-currency allocation. To
circumvent the shortage of currency, compensation trade
deals are struck, in which plant, machinery and credit are
paid for by long-term delivery of the product.

Allocations of funds to the ministries are made by the
State Planning Committee in conjunction with the State
Committee for Science and Technology and the Ministry
for Foreign Trade. The allocations form part of the five-year
plan, a subsection of which is the annual plan. The annual
plan for the following year is generally drawn up in October/
November. At this time the foreign-trade organizations are
able to discuss with reasonable certainty what they will be
in a position to buy. This does not mean that business cannot
be transacted at other times of the year. Purchases can be
authorised at any time provided that funds are available
within the allocations. November to March is often a particularly fruitful and active period for major commercial
negotiations.

RESEARCHING IN EASTERN EUROPE

Question   In view of Eastern bloc countries being planned economies, what is the best way to carry out preliminary market
research?

There is an important difference between researching in the
East and researching in the West. Soviet organizations do
not usually disclose the statistical, technical and economic
information that makes up the 'secondary' or published data
of Western markets. In the West it is this information that
allows decisions to be made about market entry, product
specification, pricing levels and the right distribution
channels to employ for companies new to the market.

There is another significant difference. Identifying a

product gap, or the opportunity to supply existing products at substantially lower prices or higher quality, is simply not a factor that influences the placing of purchase contracts.

Research must therefore be restricted to the information that is available. But there is room for an innovative approach. For example, the marketing planning of a diamond merchant would be helped by the knowledge of Soviet diamond production, stocks, product design and development. If it were known, for instance, that large stocks existed that were to be released on the world market, pricing levels would be affected.

Such information is not published and is not available. A Western scientist writing to a scientist in Russia about a diamond-related problem is able to exchange and discuss ideas freely. A spin-off is information gathered about the nature and extent of diamond technology and related matters.

An expedient desk-research approach to Eastern bloc countries is as follows:

Embargo list   The Department of Trade provides a classification of permitted goods in respect of East West trade. Specific export licences are required for goods listed on Schedule 1 of the Export of Goods (Control) Order 1980.

Statistical research data   Published information from Eastern bloc countries falls into three major catgories:

- Production and consumption targets. The targets are set out in annual and in five-year plans. They are published by each country. The targets are the central planning core of the economies.
- Production plans. The five-year plans give a general outline of the targeted output and the expansion of capacity for each industrial branch and service sector of the economy. The difference between the targeted output of each year of the plan and the targeted consumption during the year for the same product is an important factor when estimating the volume of the imports. It is by studying the previous and current five-year plans that long-term growth potential for imported goods can be deduced. The foreign-trade plan is not published as such, but the import and export

plans of specific industries and economic sectors are sometimes summarized in the trade press of each Eastern country.

- Bilateral trade agreements. Analysis of the agreements identifies products and their supply sources. It is unlikely that imports of similar goods will be made from Western sources.

Exhibitions Visiting exhibitions is an excellent method of gathering information. Participating in exhibitions is equally a first-class method of promoting products and services in Eastern bloc countries. The venue becomes a meeting place for technical specialists, end users, engineers and ministry officials. Contact with such people is often difficult elsewhere.

Shopping lists The ministry organizing exhibitions – in Russia it is Expocentr – usually issues a list of the particular goods in which there is interest. For goods not appearing on that list, or elsewhere specified, there are no short-term prospects of sales.

Opportunities to influence technical specialists and end users particularly arise at exhibitions and are important initial steps towards generating medium- and long-term sales. Because Eastern countries are centrally planned, there is long lead time between the initial contact with the foreign-trade organization and the placing of a purchase contract. Funds must be allocated for all purchases and the planning process can take years.

Exporters must be patient. Also they should always liaise with the commercial office of the British embassy, providing copies of correspondence concerning appointments and negotiations.

OVERCOMING DIFFICULTIES

Question **What is the best approach for a would-be exporter to Eastern Europe?**

The starting point for a would-be exporter to Russia or one of the Eastern European countries is to contact the trade delegation in the UK or the relevant embassy. It is necessary to identify the ministry and the foreign-trade organization concerned with the exporter's industry and products.

This information is obtainable from a published list of the products and services imported by each of the Eastern European foreign trade organizations. The addresses of the organizations together with the names and addresses of each of the industrial ministries in the socialist countries of Eastern Europe have been meticulously compiled by the London Chamber of Commerce. The name of the booklet is *Trade Contacts in Eastern Europe* (published by Kogan Page, London, 1980).

The company should send letters to the appropriate ministry and to the foreign-trade organization giving full technical information. The letters should describe the company's capacity, experience and track record in communist and in industrialized countries. The information should be confined to hard, detailed and technical fact, because advertising puff has no impact. There is an advantage in translating letters into Russian: it increases the chances of product specification and data being read. Multiple copies are helpful too.

Purchases in hard currency are the responsibility of the foreign-trade organizations. They negotiate and sign all contracts with foreign firms. They issue enquiries, based on the specifications drawn up by the ministries and are responsible for ensuring that the goods purchased meet those specifications. Public tenders are not advertised. Enquiries are sent to selected firms, usually those that are well known to the foreign trade organization.

There is not always an immediate response to the preliminary overtures made by an exporter. Patience and persistence are appropriate. To follow up the initial letters, a visit is expedient – indeed vital. Exporters can make use of regular missions organized by different chambers of commerce and other organizations. These have BOTB support and offer administrative advantages, together with the benefits of travelling in the company of seasoned exporters.

In addition to the prospecting visit, there are two other valuable activities within the overseas market.

Exhibiting at an exhibition Participation at an exhibition is an excellent method of promoting company products and services. Lists of venues are published through the appropriate foreign trade corporation and are available through BOTB. Immediate results are not necessarily to be expected. But the contacts that are made with the visiting specialists and officials are the bedrock of future business. The contacts can influence future buying decisions even to the extent of influencing the technical specification of future enquiries. Since engineers, technical specialists, the end users, and the officials who attend the exhibitions have very limited opportunities to travel abroad, exhibitions provide the chance of displaying product equipment with which they are unfamiliar.

Mounting a technical seminar or symposium For the appropriate technological product or service, the seminar or symposium is a very good method of promotion. For example, when the product or service is unfamiliar to the engineers of the country, it provides an opportunity to effect an introduction. It is also an opportunity to influence the decision-makers at the ministries when they identify and plan future technology imports. Seminars and symposia are arranged through the state committees for science and technology, through the foreign trade corporations, or through the offices of a foreign company or bank that is accredited in the country.

DEGREES OF DIFFERENCE

Question Does an exporter transact business with all Eastern bloc countries in the same way?

As regards business with Russia, Romania, East Germany, Czechoslovakia, Poland and Hungary, there are similarities and there are differences. In all countries, business is centrally planned and administered. All are short of hard currency with which to make purchases from the West. All welcome opportunities for transacting business through barter, counter purchase and compensation trading. In addition, all seek to increase trade though licence agreement – where royalties are earned through licensing out and technology is acquired through licensing in.

There are differences in terms of the amount of trading freedom that some of the countries permit. For example, under Poland's economic reform programme an increasing number of individual Polish companies are given their own foreign-trading rights. The companies can import and export autonomously without recourse to a foreign-trade organization. Similarly in Hungary, there are now some 170 companies that have been granted foreign-trading rights with varying degrees of authority to trade overseas independently.

Another point of difference is the extent of freedom for agency representations. For example, under regulations issued in 1971, Romania permits foreign firms to establish a trading office in Romania. The staff may be expatriate, Romanian or a mixture of both. In Hungary there are eleven state-owned agency companies operating. Since 1974 the agency companies have been allowed to establish special departments manned by expatriate staff to deal specifically with an overseas exporter's interests.

Clearly each country of the Eastern bloc is at a different level of trading liberalization. Pre-export research should therefore comprehensively identify the terms, conditions and opportunities for trading.

SUMMARY

Question In what ways does trading with Eastern markets differ from trading with Western markets?

Answer The most significant difference in trading patterns between East and West is that in Eastern Europe the economies are centrally planned. In the West the market forces of supply and demand are free to find their own levels.

Question COMECON is associated with trade with the East. What does it mean?

Answer COMECON, also known as CMEA, is the Council for Mutual Economic Assistance. East Germany, USSR,

Romania, Czechoslovakia, Poland, Bulgaria, Hungary, Cuba
and Vietnam have member status: Yugoslavia, attends
meetings as an observer.

Question In view of Eastern bloc countries being planned
economies, what is the best way to carry out preliminary market
research?

Answer Research is of necessity restricted to very limited
published information augmented by observation and
discussion with party officials, end users and technical
specialists in the market-place and at local exhibitions.

Question What is the best approach for a would-be exporter
to Eastern Europe?

Answer The starting point of exports to the East is identifying the foreign-trade organization concerned with the
exporter's industry and products. This should be followed
by patience, persistence and frequent visits to the market.
Full use of the British government support service increases
business opportunities.

Question Does an exporter transact business with all Eastern
bloc countries in the same way?

Answer There are similarities and differences between the
different Eastern countries. Compared to Western trading
there are marked degrees of liberalization between the countries.

APPENDIX TO CHAPTER 11: SOURCES, ADVICE, ASSISTANCE AND INFORMATION

Directories

Register of Commercial Houses Trading with Eastern Europe

(East European Trade Council, 25 Victoria Street, London SW1X 0EX).

Trade Contacts in Eastern Europe (London Chamber of Commerce and Industry, 69 Cannon Street, London EC4N 5AB).

Czechoslovakia

Chamber of Commerce of Czechoslovakia
Argentinska 38
Prague 7

East Germany

Ministry for Foreign Trade
(Ministerium für Aussendhandel),
1080 Berlin
Unter den Linden 44–60.

The International Trade Centre
(Internationales Handelszentrum),
1086 Berlin,
Friedrichstrasse.

Chamber of Commerce
(Kammer für Aussenhandel – KFA)
1100 Berlin
SchonholzerStrasse 10–11

Hungary

Hungarian Chamber of Commerce
Budapest V
Kossuth Lajos ter 6/7

Hungarian Foreign Trade Bank Ltd
Budapest V
Szent Istvn ter 11

Poland

The Polish Chamber of Foreign Trade
00–950 Warszawa,
ul. Trebacka 4

The Ministry of Foreign Trade
(Ministerstwo Handlu Zagranicznego)
00–950 Warszawa

Romania

Ministry of Foreign Trade and International Economic
Co-operation
(Ministerul Comertului Exterior si Cooperarii)
14 Bd Republicii, Bucharest

The Chamber of Commerce of the Socialist Republic of
Romania
Boulevard N. Balcescu 22,
Bucharest

USSR (Soviet foreign-trade organizations)

V/O Almazyuvelirexport
Zubovski Bulvar 25, Korpus 1
Moscow 119021

Imports Precious stones and metals.

V/O Aviaexport
32/34 Smolenskaya Sennaya Ploshchad Entrance 4
Moscow 121200

Imports Aircraft, aircraft engines, spare parts, instruments
and equipment, airport equipment, aircraft repair shops.

V/D Avtoexport
Volkhonka Ulitsa 14
Moscow 119902

Imports Cars, lorries trucks, buses, motorcycles, scooters, cycles, spares, garage equipment.

V/O Avtopromimport
50/2 Pyatnitskaya Ulitsa
Moscow 109017

Imports Equipment for the motor vehicle industry.

V/O Electronorgtechnikka
ChaikovskogoUlitsa 11a
Moscow 121834

Imports Computers, vacuum and semiconductor instruments, radio components.

V/O Exportkhleb
32/34 Smolenskaya Sennaya Ploshchad Entrance 1
Moscow 121200

Imports Grains, pulses, flour, seeds, plants.

V/O Exportles
Trubnikovskiy Per 19
Moscow 121803

Imports Industrial paper, cardboard, viscose pulp, allied timber products.

V/O Exportlyon
Ulitsa Arkhitektora Vlasova 33
Moscow 117393

Imports Raw cotton, wool, camel hair, jute, jute products, silk, fabrics.

V/O Litsenzintoro
Minskaya Ulitsa 11
Moscow 121108

Negotiates licensing agreements.

V/O Machinoimport
32/34 Smolenskaya Sennaya Ploshchad Entrance 2
Moscow 121200

Imports Electric/gas welding equipment, power electrotechnical, drilling, oil refining and dressing equipment, pumps, compressor, hoisting and handling equipment, railway rolling stock.

V/O Mashpriborintorg
32/34 Smolenskaya Sennaya Ploshchard
Moscow 121200

Imports Cinematograph, communications, seismic and geophysical equipment; measuring instruments, nuclear engineering devices; electrical and radio measuring instruments; control appliances, optical, geodetic and hydrometeorological appliances; adding machines; analytical and testing machines; typewriters, scales, watches, cameras, TV and radio sets, tape recorders, radio equipment.

V/O Medexport
Ulitsa Kakhovka 31
Moscow 113461

Imports Drugs, medicines, pharmaceuticals, medical and veterinary equipment.

12 Exporting to Japan: a special case

Before reading the chapter, answer the following test questions. The answers are worked through in the text. Question and answer are collected together at the end of the chapter as a summary.

QUESTIONS

What are the pros and cons of trying to export to Japan?

What is the best way to research the Japanese market from the UK?

What steps to doing business with Japan are likely to lead to success?

What practical rules should be obeyed by the businessman on a trip to Japan?

What is the marketing mix appropriate to the Japanese market?

Chapter 12 synopsis
- Why export?
- UK desk research
- How to start
- How to behave
- Getting the formula right

WHY EXPORT?

Question **What are the pros and cons of trying to export to Japan?**

Japan is a large market. In terms of population the estimate of numbers in 1984 was 120 million people. But they speak a different language. They are also a long way away. Japan is a worthwhile market, but there are difficulties that must be balanced against the opportunities for profit and expansion.

Incentives for trading with Japan

- The Japanese economy is the second largest in the world outside of the Eastern bloc. It is about half the size of the EEC and 40 per cent of the size of the US economy.
- The income per head is greater than the income per head in the UK.
- The Gross Domestic Product is three times as large as that of the UK.
- There are about 8 000 trading companies in Japan, many handling a wide range of goods and services.
- There are some twelve department store groups with main stores of substantial size.

Disincentives to trading with Japan

- Japan is a long way from Europe.
- The language is difficult and different. Although many people in Japan speak English – which is the business language – very many do not understand it. Confusion arises even with Japanese–English interpreters.
- The decision-making process is different from that with which Western businessmen are familiar. Decisions are reached by consensus amongst all those involved in projected activities. In the West questions are asked; answers are given, or found, to those questions; a decision is then made either to go ahead, or to do nothing, or to suspend decision-making meantime. However, in Japan, questions are asked; answers are given; the

same questions are then asked by others. It can happen again and again, sometimes with long delays that are infuriating to those unfamiliar with the Japanese decision-making process. The decision-making system is known as *ringi*. There is usually a document or *ringisho* prepared by someone at middle-management level. It carries relevant data and recommendations. The proposals are then passed for consideration to all in the company, concerned in any way – from the lowest section manager to the managing director. There are many conferences and meetings in respect of the decision to be made. If there is any disagreement, the problems are thrashed out. If necessary, the whole procedure is started again from the beginning. When a policy is ultimately adopted all have been involved, but no one person is specifically responsible for the decision that has been made.

- The Japanese consumer is exacting in terms of product quality. Total reliability and immaculate packaging are demanded. Japanese manufacturers themselves work towards a 'zero defect' rate of manufacture. There is always meticulous co-operation between the manufacturer and the component supplier to eradicate manufacturing defect problems – in the interest of the Japanese consumer.

- The Japanese consumer is extremely loyal to existing suppliers. Outside of the department store trade, the consumer buys in small quantities from the local family-owned 'corner shop' providing personal service. The lure of discounted bulk shopping is disregarded in favour of existing personal relationships. In terms of breaking into the Japanese market, time and patience are prerequisites.

- The Japanese have difficulty in saying 'No'. Because of their tradition of courtesy and respect, the Japanese find it almost impossible to say 'No' directly. They are likely to agree rather than offend the foreign visitor; also, 'Yes' may only mean 'Yes, I understand your question/request', even though there is no intention of implementing their agreement. This causes difficulties. Businessmen have returned to their home country believing that deals have been struck, when in fact the reverse is true.

UK DESK RESEARCH

Question **What is the best way to research the Japanese market from the UK?**

Japan is a large, sophisticated consumer market. The research approach is therefore little different from other large consumer markets. The research yield – the findings – however, are likely to be different. Habit and tradition have a very strong influence on buying patterns. There are therefore difficulties for the would-be supplier. But surveys, products tests, trial marketing launches are able to indicate what product and service opportunities do exist. It is important to gather a general picture of the market. In this way gaps can be identified together with any possibilities of creating a new market.

The market surveys themselves are peculiar to Japan. They are often carried out by the local retail shops with the help of their distributors. Small gifts are given to most people concerned with the project to establish the 'right' relationship.

Preliminary research starts in the home market. Much market-related data is available in the UK. There are four organizations that are the most useful contact points for securing Anglo–Japanese trade and economic information:

JETRO – LONDON (Japan External Trade Organization) The primary aim of JETRO is to promote international trade, in accordance with the Japanese government policy of free trade. The organization is an enterprising, non-profit making, trade promotional body. There are full resources of experience and marketing know-how, reinforced by JETRO offices in thirty areas of Japan.

JETRO personnel are completely familiar with Japanese business practice, and with the complex distribution system within Japan. Information can therefore be given on the markets for specific products and services.

There are also opportunities for assistance with a product launch. JETRO circulates information about the product in the *JETRO Trade Enquiry*. This weekly trade bulletin has a circulation of 20 000 import agents and distributors in Japan. At least once a month a special issue entitled 'Exporting to Japan' features photographs of promising products.

EJU – BOTB (Exports to Japan Unit – British Overseas Trade Board)   There is a special BOTB unit for the Japanese market. It is warranted by the size of the market and the potential for exporters to do good business. The unit is staffed by people with first-hand knowledge of Japan and the way to transact business there.

Through the unit, exporters are able to work closely with the Commercial Department of the British Embassy in Tokyo and the British Consulate General in Osaka. There is also active contact with the Japanese business community in the UK – with opportunities for evaluating product potential in the UK, before going out to Japan.

Japanese Chamber of Commerce and Industry in the UK   The Chamber offers the range of services one would expect:

- information on Japanese companies
- library
- telephone enquiry service.

British Chamber of Commerce in Japan. Advice is available from experienced, skilled, Japanese-speaking expatriates.

Names, addresses and telephone numbers are given in the appendix to this chapter.

HOW TO START

Question **What steps to doing business with Japan are likely to lead to success?**

There are four important steps to doing business with Japan:

Step 1 is preliminary market research in the UK. Findings,

trends, reports – opinions from Japanese buying offices in the UK – suggest to the would-be exporter that there are chances to do business. This is encouraging. But unlike some other markets, trade cannot be expected to start immediately. Japanese business is transacted through personal relationships. Such relationships must be established. Time is of the essence. But lots and lots of time.

There is no hard-and-fast rule. It can take five years, even ten, to reach profitability. Sometimes it is much quicker. An unattractive small initial order is not necessarily a preliminary trial order to precede bulk instructions. It can be the foundation stone of a supplier–customer relationship that grows slowly on trust and co-operation. The way business is transacted in Japan is through established channels.

Step 2 is a fact-finding trip to Japan. Introductions are made. Field research facts are gathered. An understanding is gained of the Japanese life-style and of the real ways in which Japanese thinking and living is different from the familiar patterns of the home country.

On the fact-finding initial trip, impatience must be curbed. It is not the Western-style opportunity for immediate business negotiations. The Japanese themselves practise this approach to business overseas. An employee of a Japanese trading company assigned to a Latin American country was told before leaving Tokyo not to engage in business for one year. His brief initially was simply to learn the language and to get to know how the local businessmen and consumers lived.

Step 3 is a commitment to meeting Japanese standards. Japanese buyers demand perfection. There is no question of batch variation in colour, size, shape, quality, weight, specification, packaging or labelling. All goods must precisely replicate the sample that preceded them. Deliveries that are overdue extinguish a business relationship.

Business with Japan is a long-term commitment. Profits follow from the creation of trust. Building up that trust is slow and arduous. Decisions from Japan are formulated through concensus and appears very time-consuming from a Western point of view.

Step 4 is deciding the method of entry. Overall, there are four methods of entry into the Japanese market for direct exports:

- Selling through department stores. Direct sales to department stores and to store groups cuts out middlemen. Opportunities are attractive, certainly as a test of the demand, but not as the route to very large volume sales. There are limitations. All store buyers importing directly will demand exclusivity. There are therefore constraints on potential volume.
- Selling piggy back through manufacturers. The exporter provides a product or products that are complementary to the manufacturer's own product range. There are many advantages. The manufacturer has his own distribution channels. He is expert in the marketing and promotion appropriate to his industry. An example is Budweiser beer imported by the whisky manufacturer Suntory.
- Sogo Shosha – the large general trading companies. The nine largest trading companies known as *sogo shosha* handle a wide range of goods. They are very large companies indeed. Mitsubishi Corporation is the biggest, with sales in 1983 of £50 billion. Over £16 billion of this represented imports into Japan.

   The trading companies concentrate on high-volume, high-value imports. Working closely with Japanese manufacturers they also handle Japanese exports and international trading. Because of their size they may not fall into the category of first option for the small-to medium-sized British exporter. All of the companies have a presence in London. Names and addresses are available from the Exports to Japan Unit of BOTB.
- Specialist trading companies agents. This method of entry may be the most productive for the would-be exporter. The companies are small but have access to the very large market. Being small they are perhaps likely to have a more pressing need to succeed than the giant trading companies. The names and addresses of potential agents are obtainable through the Exports to Japan Unit.

HOW TO BEHAVE

Question What practical rules should be obeyed by the business-man on a trip to Japan?

Foreign visitors to Japan are faced with a nation living in a different culture and speaking a different language. To do business with the Japanese it is necessary to learn and to adopt their codes of behaviour. Subordinating Western flamboyance and aggression is a necessary measure of humility. And humility is valued by the Japanese so highly that it is surpassed by only one other virtue – patience.

Business cards Visitors to Japan should take a copious supply of business calling cards. The cards are called *meishi*. They are an integral part of business introductions, which are themselves a part of the business fabric. One side of the card is printed in English, the other in Japanese. The card is important because it says clearly who you are, what you sell and what kind of company you represent. Status is all in Japan. Seniority of rank in Japan is linked closely with age and the years of service in the company.

When introduced, Japanese usually immediately present their name card and repeat their name. When receiving a card they solemnly and respectfully study it for a few moments. Once a card has been exchanged in Japan, it is kept and filed, and is the basis of the future relationships that are so important. Once cards are exchanged, a person is no longer a stranger. In Japan, business is not done with strangers. Telephoning cold to make an appointment does not succeed.

Company brochure For the business visitor to Japan a company brochure or product catalogue is as important as the visiting card. It is a method of demonstrating the credibility of the company. With a preliminary fact-finding mission, a decision may be taken to dispense with a Japanese printed version, for reasons of cost. But the visitor should consider ways of describing and demonstrating track record and performance. Visitors should invest themselves with the highest status compatible with conscience.

Make use of an interpreter   Before a business meeting, run over the subject-matter/product vocabulary with the interpreter. Japanese and English are very difficult languages. Large numbers/sums of money are particular pitfalls.

Written confirmation   After a meeting of importance check over with the interpreter and with the other side that the points discussed are fully understood. Always reinforce a business discussion with a written confirmation of what has been said.

Never argue or shout   Such behaviour is alien to the essential courtesy of the Japanese relationship. Disagreement must be formulated in phrases of impeccable diplomacy.

Enjoy, and subsequently return, the hospitality and friendliness that is afforded the visitor. Entertainment is often lavish. After the visit the relationship that has been established can be sustained by letters and postcards and simple gifts. The objective is to reinforce the pleasant memories of the visit. Reciprocal interest is standard practice amongst the Japanese. Not to conform leaves a potentially damaging aftertaste of misunderstanding.

GETTING THE FORMULA RIGHT

Question   What is the marketing mix appropriate to the Japanese market?

Japan is a very special case. It is a tough, exacting market. With determined application it is also profitable. Much thought and attention is required for each of the variables that the marketer controls:

Product

It is most likely that the product must be differentiated to suit Japanese taste. In clothing, for example, the need is obvious. British sizing is not appropriate to the Japanese form, although the printing of the label sizing is a different matter. In the Italian market, Aquascutum, which had provided continental sizing for their exported men's suits, were asked by the importers to revert to traditional English sizes. The size label itself was part of the up-market image of elegance and fine tailoring.

Guidance on consumer needs should be obtained from the importer or partner or agent, through whom or with whom business is being transacted. Taste, appetite and tolerance levels of the Japanese consumer are different in many ways to the Western counterpart. Furthermore, the Japanese consumer is hypercritical and demanding in product quality, function, design and packaging.

There are a few examples where the exporter knows best and does not take advice. McDonalds is one. The product format is not changed – and the outlet on the Ginza in Tokyo is the most successful worldwide.

Price

Because of the complex distribution system in Japan, imported goods reach the consumer at a price greatly inflated from the landed cost. Most potential exporters aim at the top end of the market. At this position, price is important but it is also an integral part of the product image. A branded whisky manufacturer reduced the selling price of his product: the effect was counter to expectation; sales dropped. The reduction in price adversely influenced the status of the product in the perception of the consumer.

Price is important. It is a function of negotiations between importer and exporter. There are also a number of ways of keeping the prices down:

- Exporting in bulk and packaging in Japan. In addition to reduced distribution and handling costs, there can be reduction in tariff rates.
- Incorporation of Japanese component parts.
- Third-country production where labour costs are cheaper.

Place

The Japanese distribution system is highly complex. The

reason is the structure of consumer demand and purchasing. Apart from the department stores and supermarkets, the major part of Japanese purchases are made from small family-owned businesses. Consumer purchases tend to be made on a day-to-day basis in small quantities. Personal relationships between retail outlet and consumer are thereby reinforced.

Primary, secondary and tertiary wholesalers purchase from the importer. Each has its own specialized network of distribution channels. Although the merchandise becomes more expensive because of the number of middlemen in the channels, the consumer accepts this as a price to pay for service.

The Japanese customer is supreme. He expects same-day delivery, free repairs, free samples and guaranteed reliability. Much thought should be given by the exporter to the distribution paths to be adopted. Advice should be taken. It is unwise, if not impossible, to export alone. With products that need little after-sales service, the diversity of the distribution system provides several levels of distributors to offer the product to the purchasers.

Promotion

Japanese product exhibitions and trade fairs are very important promotional activities. There are two types:

- Exhibitions organized and sponsored by government – Japanese or British. An important feature is free participation. Exhibitions intended exclusively for foreign exhibitors are particularly useful to would-be exporters. Opportunities are thus presented to assess the market and find a Japanese import agent.
- General trade fairs open to all Japanese. The latter are organized most commonly by trade associations. They are nation wide. They are attended in very large numbers. But many trade fairs do not allow foreign companies to participate independently. Cooperation is therefore necessary with a Japanese importer or partner.

Trade fairs in Japan are not the same as those held in

the West. The emphasis is different. In the West the fairs provide an opportunity for buyer and seller to meet and to agree business. There are also peripheral benefits – an agent finding a principal, new product launches, the monitoring of industry progress.

In Japan the objectives of the trade fair are:

- collection of information relating to new products, market movements, new technology, new companies with whom to establish business relations.
- exchange of goodwill with existing customers, and with industry officialdom

At the end of a fair the businessman has few orders, if any, and a large pile of visiting cards. Japanese visitors to exhibition stands take back the name cards they have collected, together with all the product samples and catalogues and brochures. These are subsequently and slowly considered and digested by the visitor companies. If there is interest, contact is made, but a long time afterwards by Western standards.

To be effective, advertising in Japan must have a big budget. Because of the sophisticated and idiosyncratic market, the campaign is best planned by experts. New products are judged by a combination of the impact of the advertisement copy, media exposure, packaging, quality and price. Status is all important, so packing and promotion and copy should strive to provide the most up-market image.

Service

Products that require a great deal of post-sales service normally have a service company operated directly by the manufacturer. Customers specify to the manufacturer the degree of service levels required. The level is extremely high. Buyers are often informed of the home telephone numbers of service personnel so that customers can call them at any time of the day or night. There is no question of periods off for holidays. When service is part of the package, it has to be immaculate – otherwise business dies. When consumer durable products are unfamiliar to the end users, arrangements are necessary to provide training in product usage.

It is the intention of this chapter to identify the hurdles that impede the progress of the would-be exporter to Japan. But the initial path is uphill, costly, frustrating and time-consuming. The British Chamber of Commerce in Japan recently published a selection of the many British success stories. They are reproduced below:

- A giftware and china company boosted exports from £0.5 m to £4m.

  How? By setting up its own importing business, thus showing commitment and offering better service.

- A British-owned electronics subsidiary built up a £40m market with unique direct-to-retailer and OEM sales. It now dominates its market segment. Strong patents also support a major licensing operation.

  How? Through local commitment, Japanese product merchandising, own-trained sales force and very fast service.

- A British specialist engineering supplies company dramatically increased sales to the Japanese food industry.

  How? By marketing to Japanese conditions, not British ones. Now even traditional Japanese food manufacturers use their equipment.

- A British industry gas company created a profitable $200m business through merger and takeover, and is now a major force in an important market.

  How? By developing a co-operative relationship, moving with care and talking Japanese.

- An Anglo-European joint venture industrial service company pushed sales to £2m with high profit levels in two years from start up, and now dominates specialist market.

  How? By using well-established connections and taking full advantage of strong patent cover in its pricing.

SUMMARY

Question **What are the pros and cons of trying to export to Japan?**

Answer Japan is a large rich market, with massive consumer spending power. It is an idiosyncratic market, demanding product quality, design, packaging, reliability and service of the highest level. Japanese do not behave according to the patterns understood and practised in the Western world. Would-be exporters must learn to adapt to the Japanese code of practice, leading to business profitability in the medium to long term.

Question **What is the best way to research the Japanese market from the UK?**

Answer Because of the potential of the Japanese market, there is much governmental and semi-governmental support for export research. The starting point for would-be exporters is with four organizations: the Japan External Trade Organization – London; the Exports to Japan Unit of the British Overseas Trade Board; the Japanese Chamber of Commerce and Industry in the UK; and the British Chamber of Commerce in Japan. All addresses and telephone numbers are given in the appendix to this chapter.

Question **What steps to doing business with Japan are likely to succeed?**

Answer There are four important steps to take:
1 Undertake preliminary market research.
2 Make a fact-finding, contact-making visit to Japan.
3 Make a commitment to meeting the long-term Japanese approach to business, rethinking the application of Western business methods.
4 Decide, with informed guidance, on the most appropriate method of market entry.

Question **What practical rules should be obeyed by a businessman on a trip to Japan?**

Answer Businessmen travelling to Japan should

- take with them a copious supply of visiting cards printed in Japanese and English
- carefully record and retain all visiting cards given in exchange as they form the basis of future relationships
- make available products, samples and catalogues demonstrating the size, credibility and track record of the company
- thoroughly rehearse any technical vocabulary to be used by interpreters at a business meeting
- confirm the basis of all discussions in writing and ensure that mutual understanding actually took place
- avoid all direct confrontation and argument, notwithstanding the circumstances.
- Repay all hospitality with appropriate gratitude and appreciation.

Question   What is the marketing mix appropriate to the Japanese market?

Answer   The mix of product, price, place, promotion and service must be thoroughly differentiated from that of the home market to match the precise and demanding needs of the Japanese market.

APPENDIX TO CHAPTER 12: SOURCES OF ADVICE, ASSISTANCE AND INFORMATION

Japan External Trade Organization (JETRO) – London
Leconfield House
Curzon Street
London W1Y 7FB
Tel.: 01 493 7226
Fax: 01 491 7570

Exports to Japan Unit – British Overseas Trade Board (EJU – BOTB)
1 Victoria Street
London SW1H 0ET

Tel.: 01 215 4805 (tariff and general enquiries)
    01 215 4803 (industrial products)
    01 215 4802 (consumer products)
    01 215 5426 (exhibitions and missions)
    01 215 4799 (industrial co-operation)

Japanese Chamber of Commerce and Industry in the UK
c/o Mitsubishi Corporation (odd years)
Bow Bells House
Bread Street
London EC4M 9BQ
Tel.: 01 822 0022
Telex: 885531 or 888171
Cable: Mitsui London EC4
Fax: 01 236 2130

c/o Mitsui and Co Ltd (even years)
Temple Court
11 Queen Victoria Street
London EC4N 4SB
Tel.: 01 600 1777

British Chamber of Commerce in Japan
3F, Kowa Bldg, No. 1
11–41, Akasaka 1-chome
Minato-ku
Tokyo 107
Japan
Tel.: 505 1734

Glossary

ASEAN	Association of South East Asian Nation
B/E	bill of exchange
B/L	bill of lading
BOTB	British Overseas Trading Board
BSI	British Standards Institution
BTN	Brussels tariff nomenclature
CAD	cash against documents
C&F	cost and freight
CAM	Communications, Advertising and Marketing Education Foundation
CI	consular invoice
CIF	cost insurance freight
CIFC	cost insurance freight and commission
CIP	freight or carriage and insurance paid to
CO	certificate of origin
COC	cash on collection
COP	cash on presentation
CTC	combined transport convention
CWO	cash with order
DA	documents against acceptance
DAF	delivered at frontier
DOP	freight or carriage paid to
DP	documents against payment
DR	dock receipt
E&OE	errors and ommissions excepted
ECGD	Export Credits Guarantee Department
EEC	European Economic Community
EFTA	European Free Trade Area
ExQ	ex quay
ExS	ex ship

ExW	ex works
FAS	free alongside
FMCG	Fast moving consumer goods
FOA	F.O.B. Airport
FOB	free on board
FOR	free on rail
FOT	free on truck
franco	delivered to customer's premises duty paid
FPA	free from particular average
FRC	free carrier
FTZ	free-trade zone
GA	general average
GATT	General Agreement on Tariffs and Trade
IAA	International Advertising Association
IATA	International Air Transport Association
ICLC	irrevocable confirmed letter of credit
ILD	Inernational Labour Organization
IMF	International Monetary Fund
LAFTA	Latin America Free Trade Area
LTL	less than truck load
NEDO	National Economic Development Office
OECD	Organization for Economic Development and Co-operation
OGL	open general licence
OPEC	Organization for Petroleum Exporting Countries
SDR	special drawing rights
SIC	Standard industrial classification
SITC	Standard International Trade Classification
TIR	Transports Interntionales Routiers
TT	telegraph transfer
UKTA	United Kingdom Trade Agency
UNCC	United Nations Country Code
UNCTAD	United Nations Conference on Trade and Development
UNESCO	United Nations Educational Scientific and Cultural Organization
UNIDO	United Nations Industrial Development Organization
VAT	Value Added Tax
WA	with average

Bibliography

BOTB International Directory of Published Market Research,
   London: British Overseas Trade Board, 1984
Brown, R.H., *Marine Insurance Principles,* Vol 1, London:
   Witherby, 1978
Cannon, Tom, *Basic Marketing,* Holt Business Texts 1982
Croner's Reference Book for Exporters, London: Croner, 1986
Export Handbook: Services for British Exporters, London:
   British Overseas Trade Board
Hibbert, E.P., *The Principles & Practice of Export Marketing,*
   London: Heinemann, 1985
Hill, Malcolm, R., *Export Marketing of Capital Goods to
   the Socialist Countries of Eastern Europe,* Aldershot: Gower,
   1978
Hints to Exporters, London: British Overseas Trade Board
Incoterms, (International Rules for the Interpretation of
   Trade Terms), Paris: International Chamber of Commerce
   No 350, 1980
Ishiwata, K., (ed.), *Export to Japan Guidebook for UK
   Exporters,* London: Jetro, 1986
Majaro, Simon, *International Marketing: A Strategic
   Approach,* 2nd edition, London: Allen & Unwin, 1983
Majaro, Simon *Marketing in Perspective,* George Allen and
   Unwin 1982
Noonan, C., *Practical Export Management,* London: George
   Allen & Unwin, 1985
Piercy, Nigel, *Export Strategy: Markets and Competition,*
   London: Allen & Unwin, 1982
Ricks, David A., *Big Business Blunders,* Homewood, IL: Dow
   Jones-Irwin, 1983

Schmitthoff, C., *Agency Agreements in the Export Trade*,
London: Institute of Export, 1980

Schmitthoff, C., *The Export Trade*, London: Stevens & Sons,
1980

The Effective Export Department, London :SITPRO, 1982

Uniform Customs and Practice for Documentary Credits, Paris:
International Chamber of Commerce No 400, 1983

Walker, A.G., *Export Practice and Documentation*, Sevenoaks:
Newnes - Butterworths, 1977

Walsh, L., *International Marketing*, Plymouth: Macdonald
& Evans, 1981

Index